Political Economy of Algeria

Algeria, the largest country in North Africa, is geopolitically significant due to its strategic location and natural resources. Despite its potential, the country remains entrenched in a rent-based economy, heavily dependent on hydrocarbon exports, a situation that has persisted since its independence in 1962.

This book provides a comprehensive analysis of Algeria's complex politico-economic system, focusing on its rentier and extractivist nature. The study examines the historical evolution of Algeria's economy, beginning with the ambitious yet ultimately unsuccessful industrialisation efforts of the 1960s and 1970s. This failure led to the country's specialisation in the extraction and export of hydrocarbons. Subsequent reforms aimed at transitioning to a market economy have failed to break the country's dependency on oil revenues, instead deepening its rentier and extractivist characteristics. The book critically explores the limitations of applying conventional economic and political science frameworks to analyse the Algerian economy. It argues that these disciplines, developed within the context of Western capitalism, are insufficient to fully capture the unique dynamics of an economy like Algeria's, where the market plays a marginal role, and state-controlled rents dominate wealth distribution. To address these challenges, the book adopts the concept of extractivism, originally developed in Latin American contexts, to better understand the interplay between political struggles, social movements and economic practices in Algeria. It posits that Algeria is both a rentier and an extractivist state, with these two aspects reinforcing each other and hindering the development of a productive economy.

The book will be of interest to readers of political economy, Middle East and North African studies and international politics.

Ouchichi Mourad is a Professor of Political Science. He is currently a lecturer at the University of Bejaia, Algeria. Professor Ouchichi pursued academic research in economics with a specialisation in development studies and earned a PhD in political science from the Institute of Political Studies in Lyon, France.

Global Challenges in Political Economy

Taxation and Inequality in Latin America
New Perspectives on Political Economy and Tax Regimes
Edited by Philip Fehling and Hans-Jürgen Burchardt

The Political Economy of Extractivism
Global Perspectives on the Seduction of Rent
Edited by Hannes Warnecke-Berger and Jan Ickler

Global Rentier Capitalism
Theory and Development
Edited by Balihar Sanghera

The Political Economy of Elites in Latin America
Edited by Jan Ickler and Rebeca Ramos Padrón

Political Economy of Algeria
Extractivism, Rents and Populism
Ouchichi Mourad

For more information about this series, please visit: www.routledge.com/Global-Challenges-in-Political-Economy/book-series/GCPE

Political Economy of Algeria

Extractivism, Rents and Populism

Ouchichi Mourad

Routledge
Taylor & Francis Group
LONDON AND NEW YORK

First published 2026
by Routledge
4 Park Square, Milton Park, Abingdon, Oxon OX14 4RN

and by Routledge
605 Third Avenue, New York, NY 10158

Routledge is an imprint of the Taylor & Francis Group, an informa business

British Library Cataloguing-in-Publication Data
A catalogue record for this book is available from the British Library

ISBN: 978-1-041-12592-1 (hbk)
ISBN: 978-1-041-12593-8 (pbk)
ISBN: 978-1-003-66557-1 (ebk)

DOI: 10.4324/9781003665571

Typeset in Times New Roman
by KnowledgeWorks Global Ltd.

Contents

Figures

Tables

About the author

Ouchichi Mourad is a professor of political science, born on October 7, 1975, in Ath Laaziz, Bouira, Algeria. He is currently a lecturer at the University of Bejaia, Algeria. Professor Ouchichi pursued academic research in economics with a specialisation in development studies and earned a PhD in political science from the Institute of Political Studies in Lyon, France.

With a dual background in economics and political science, his research primarily explores development-related issues through the lens of institutional analysis. His scholarly work focuses particularly on the dynamics of rentier states, with a special emphasis on the North African context. He is also engaged in comparative research on the sociology of state economic practices.

Professor Ouchichi has contributed to numerous collaborative publications in both Algeria and France and has authored many scientific articles.

Foreword

Understanding Algeria's political economy requires a careful disentangling of the historical trajectories, institutional legacies, and global entanglements that have shaped its development since independence. In *Political Economy of Algeria,* Mourad Ouchichi offers *a* compelling and rigorous analysis of the country's economic and political structures through the lenses of rentierism and extractivism. This book is not only a timely contribution to the literature on North African political economy but also a profound engagement with the theoretical debates surrounding development, dependency, and the crisis of the postcolonial state.

The central thesis of the book—that Algeria embodies a dual structure of extractivist accumulation and rentier redistribution—situates the country within a broader pattern of global South economies whose developmental trajectories remain structurally constrained. What sets this study apart is its interdisciplinary ambition: Ouchichi draws from classical political economy, institutionalist economics, and critical state theory, while remaining attentive to the specific historical and political configurations that define the Algerian case.

The book is structured in a way that reflects both analytical clarity and historical depth. It begins by offering a rich theoretical overview of extractivism and the resource curse, laying the groundwork for a nuanced exploration of the Algerian experience. Subsequent chapters combine empirical data, historical periodisation, and policy analysis to map the evolution of Algeria's economic model—from the etatist ambitions of the 1960s and 70s to the liberalisation attempts of the 1990s and the more recent strategies around renewable energy. In doing so, Ouchichi demonstrates how every reform, adjustment, or innovation has ultimately failed to break the country's dependency on hydrocarbon rents.

Crucially, this book does not treat extractivism and rentierism as merely economic phenomena. Rather, it shows how these logics penetrate the political system, shaping social contracts, enabling populist governance, and reproducing authoritarian rule. Ouchichi convincingly argues that the Algerian state, insulated by external rents and unaccountable to productive forces within society, has transformed the economy into an administrative mechanism for political control. This fusion of rent-based redistribution and political domination explains why diversification has failed and why reformist rhetoric often masks a deeper continuity.

Particularly noteworthy is the final chapter, which tackles the pressing question of Algeria's green transition. Can renewable energy projects provide a path out of extractivism? Or are we witnessing a new phase of rentier adaptation, one that recycles old dependencies under the banner of sustainability? By introducing the concept of "green rents," the book opens a crucial debate on the geopolitics of the energy transition and the risk of neo-extractivist reproduction.

This work speaks not only to scholars of North Africa but also to a wider audience interested in resource governance, developmental states, and the political economy of authoritarian resilience. It invites us to rethink the categories we use to understand the global South: rather than applying imported paradigms uncritically, Ouchichi grounds his analysis in the lived contradictions of the Algerian context—its history, its institutions, its social struggles.

In a world marked by overlapping crises—economic inequality, energy insecurity, ecological collapse—*Political Economy of Algeria* reminds us that the question of how wealth is generated, distributed, and politicised remains at the heart of any emancipatory project. For Algeria, and for many countries facing similar dilemmas, the challenge is not merely to move beyond hydrocarbons, but to reimagine the very foundations of sovereignty, justice, and development.

Rachid Ouaissa, Marburg University, July 2025

Scope of the book

The reflection contained in this book is basically multidisciplinary. It spreads from economics to politics, including politics sociology of the economic practices of the State. The reason is that Algeria, the subject of this study, is a country with a rather peculiar political and economic system. It is characterised by an undifferentiated system where the fields—according to Bourdieu's meaning of that notion—are not autonomous from each other.

The economic field in Algeria is totally slotted into the political field. Consequently, the regulating rationality of that field is not submitted to the economic rules, most important of all, the law of supply and demand. There is certainly a movement of resources in Algeria, but those are not the result of the working force exploitation. It comes instead from the systematic injection of a part of the rent on the basis of political and populist criteria.

Such a situation makes the use of purely economic notions in any analytical reflection ineffective when it comes to working of the Algerian economy. As we mentioned in the introduction, the resort to politics is helpless, either. The reason is that at the heart of the political science problematic, there is the issue of the State. Except that one does not exist in Algeria; there is only a " pouvoir " disguised as the State.

That's why we were forced to fall back on the notion of extractivism, which first emerged in Latin American countries where capitalism arose within totally different circumstances from those in Western Europe. In other words, the emergence of a form of capitalism without the lightning of the Age of Reason. It is exactly the same situation as for the Algerian economy.

In putting forward the decisive role of political struggles within and against the well-established power, the contribution of social movements and environmental issues, extractivism distinguishes itself by combining both the issues set by political economics and politics. Having emphasised this, and to return to the initial problematic, it is evident that our analysis remains purely eclectic. In other words, it borrows from politics, political economics and political sociology of the economic practices of the State.

Acknowledgments

First and foremost, I would like to express my deepest gratitude to Professor Rachid Ouaïssa, without whose guidance and support this work would never have seen the light of day. This book is the outcome of a three-month academic research stay within the Extractivism Project at Philipps University of Marburg (Germany). I extend particular appreciation to my friend and colleague, Dr. Nadjia Ouali from Abderrahmane Mira University of Béjaïa, for enriching this work throughout its development.

Special thanks go to all colleagues who generously invested their time in reviewing early drafts and providing thoughtful feedback. Their collective insights have significantly strengthened this work. They will recognise themselves—may they find here my most sincere thanks.

Finally, this work is dedicated to all those who cherish justice and freedom, wherever they may be. A special thought for the prisoners of conscience from the February 22, 2019, Hirak movement.

Acronyms

AD	Algerian Dinars
ADEME	Environment and Energy Management
AEA	American Economic Association
AFREC	African Energy Commission
APN	National People's Assembly
APRUE	Algerian National Agency for the Promotion and Rationalisation of Energy Use
ARES	African Renewable Energy Society
AU	African Union
CDM	Clean Development Mechanism
CDER	Centre for the Development of Renewable Energies
CEEC	Central and Eastern European Countries
CEREFE	Commission for Renewable Energy and Energy Efficiency
CMC	Conseil de la Monnaie et du Crédit
CNC	National Consultative Council
CNES	Conseil National Économique et Social
CPE	Centrally Planned Economy
CREG	Commission for Electricity and Gas Regulation
CSP	Concentrated Solar Power
DEC	Délégués Exécutifs Communaux
DII	DESERTEC Industrial Initiative
EU	European Union
EUREC	European Renewable Energy Research Centres Agency
FFS	Front des Forces Socialistes
FIS	Front Islamique du Salut
FLN	Front de Libération Nationale
FSDRS	Special Development Fund for Southern Regions
GDP	Gross Domestic Product
GHG	Greenhouse Gases
GNP	Gross National Product
GSE	Socialist Management of Enterprises
HSC	High State Committee

IEA	International Energy Agency
IMF	International Monetary Fund
ISCC	Integrated Solar Power and Combined Cycle Plant
ISES	International Solar Energy Society
KW	kilowatt
LMC	Law on Money and Credit
LNG	Liquefied Natural Gas
LPG	Liquefied Petroleum Gas
ME	Medium Enterprises
MENA	Middle East and North Africa
MW	Megawatt
NEAL	New Energy Algeria
NGO	Non-Governmental Organisations
ONS	Office National des Statistiques
PE	Petites Entreprises
PNEREE	Programme National de Développement des Énergies Renouvelables et de l'Efficacité Énergétique
PV	Photovoltaics
RE	Renewable Energy
SAD	Stratégie Algérienne du Développement
SAP	Structural Adjustment Policy
SGP	Sociétés de Gestion de Participations
SME	Small and Medium-Sized Enterprises
Sonatrach	Société Nationale des Hydrocarbures, Recherche, Production, Transport, Transformation et Commercialisation
SONELGAZ	Société Nationale de l'Électricité et du Gaz
SSB	Sahara Solar Breeder
TPE	Toutes Petites Entreprises
TREC	Trans-Mediterranean Renewable Energy Cooperation
Twh	Térawattheure
UDES	Solar Equipment Development Unit
UDTS	Silicon Technology Development Unit
UGTA	Union Générale des Travailleurs Algériens
UNCTAD	United Nations Conference on Trade and Development
WB	World Bank
WEF	World Economic Forum
WWEA	World Wind Energy Association

General introduction

Algeria is the largest country in North Africa in terms of surface area (2,381,741 km^2), with 46.88 million inhabitants and 1,200 km of Mediterranean coastline. It shares land borders to the north-east with Tunisia, to the east with Libya, to the south with Niger and Mali, to the south-west with Mauritania and the Western Sahara, and with Morocco to the west. Its geostrategic position is of vital importance. It is at the centre of three gateways: Europe to the north, Africa to the south and the Arab world to the east. In addition to its natural wealth and youth, Algeria is a potential tourist destination par excellence. However, it remains trapped by its rentier and dependent nature. This observation is shared by all analysts and observers, and also by the political regime, which has been part of the same system since the country's independence in 1962. The official discourse on the need for a post-oil future dates back to the 1980s. Since then, successive reforms have been introduced with the official aim of breaking out of the rentier logic and building a productive economy, but the result remains the same. Worse still, as the years go by, the country is sinking deeper into the rentier and extractive logic.

Actually, at the end of the 1970s, the Algerian government carried out an economic and social review of its development model based on heavy industrialisation, as conceived and implemented in the 1960s and 1970s. The result was clear: the failure of this ambitious project led to a steady slide towards the country's specialisation in the extraction and export of hydrocarbons.

In the early 1980s, there was an initial experiment in "corrective" adjustments to this model, but without any convincing results. The proof was that as soon as oil prices collapsed in the mid-1980s, the country plunged into an unprecedented economic and financial crisis.

Along the way, towards the end of the 1980s, the country's leaders agreed to reform the economy with a view to the transition to a market economy and put an end to a number of state monopolies, including foreign trade. This experience was soon called into question, leading the country to adopt a Structural Adjustment Plan under the aegis of the IMF in the mid-1990s.

The year 2000 was characterised by the financial opulence of the state. They were also marked by the questioning of economic reforms in favour

DOI: 10.4324/9781003665571-1

of the massive and clientelist distribution of hydrocarbon revenues, which reinforced the rentier and extractivist nature of the economy. Thus, within a decade, the rentier logic has developed into a veritable rentier system.

However, as in countries with extractive economies, the model for distributing the wealth it does not create will reach objective limits. In 2014, as in 1986, with the downturn in the international oil and gas market, all the latent and patent contradictions of the Algerian economy came to light. Today, after more than four decades of reforms and counter-reforms, the Algerian economy still has the same characteristics, namely low capital profitability, heavy dependence on oil revenues for its foreign exchange earnings, and on the external market for its supplies of goods and services.

Indeed, neither the promises of accelerated, self-centred development made by President H. Boumediene in the 1970s, nor the various reform initiatives launched and implemented since the early 1980s, managed to break the "umbilical" link between the economy and oil revenues, which is proving to be a powerful factor in underdevelopment.

Our hypothesis in relation to this observation is that the Algerian economy does not operate according to the laws of the market; it is rather subject to the administrative injunctions of the State. This phenomenon has its roots at two levels. Firstly, the Algerian economy is not sufficiently developed, nor is the market advanced enough to impose its own forms of regulation, and the political field has no interest groups defending their positions (employers, trade unions, the multiple corporations). Secondly, the political system is still in a dilemma and does not want to choose between one solution and the other. On the one hand, it wants to liberalise the market to encourage local wealth creation, and on the other, it does not want to give up using the economy as a political resource. The leaders know that if they abandon the economy to the market, they will not control society, which will emancipate itself through autonomous professional corporations and political parties free from the tutelage of the administration.

Added to this is the influence of the Global North, which, in order to meet its needs, requires the countries of the South to specialise in the extraction and sale of raw materials, preferably in their raw state. This research aims to shed light on aspects of these issues.

With regard to the conceptual framework and methodological issues, the first difficulty encountered when analysing the Algerian market sphere is methodological. It relates to the conceptual framework needed to decipher the various changes in an economic field in which most of the wealth comes from an external rent, with what this implies for economic and social relations.

By virtue of its subject matter, economics appears to be the discipline best equipped to carry out this analysis: its long tradition of research into economic relations, its enrichment through the adoption of econometric models, and its apparent dominance in terms of the number of centres producing economic data and analysis—particularly those linked to international financial institutions—generally give it a privileged status in this field. However, as soon as the analysis of the Algerian development experience is launched, it comes up against a fundamental methodological problem.

This situation stems from the fact that economic science is based on postulates and categories of analysis forged in a historical situation that is totally different from that in which the Algerian commercial sphere is evolving. Indeed, as a reflection of the historical reality of capitalism, the object of study in economics is the creation and distribution of wealth through prices, the formation of which obeys the logic of supply and demand. The concepts of profit, wages, prices, etc. can only be interpreted in a historical context in which the economic sphere is autonomous, i.e. operates according to its own laws. This presupposes the existence of a political organisation that respects the autonomy of economic agents and guarantees the competitive conditions that allow the law of value to evolve. This is to underline that when it is extracted from its historical context and cut off from the political relations it establishes between economic agents, economic science—currently dominated by neo-classical approaches and the currents it inspires in the image of the monetarists—loses all its relevance.

Faced with this thorny problem, a number of economists have resigned themselves to reducing their reflections to a so-called "purely economic" analysis; in other words, limiting their field of investigation to the hypotheses of Walrasian political economy. As a result, they miss out on an essential part of reality by analysing the flow of value in the Algerian economic field from the sole perspective of the logic of markets, itself taken from the sole perspective of individual economic rationality. IMF experts and a number of Algerian economic policy designers fall into this category. This largely explains the fact that all the policies recommended for Algeria, including the Structural Adjustment Plan, have failed to trigger development. In Algeria, the market plays only a marginal role in wealth creation. The dominant sphere is that of revenues distributed by the state according to certain criteria. The question that arises, then, is what alternative an economist could resort to in order to escape this "methodological impasse."

Initially, we have attempted to turn to classical political economy. This is justified because it was classical economics, notably through Ricardo's work, that identified rents as a handicap to the dynamics of accumulation. It is also this work that has shown the ways of extinguishing rents in order to free up effective demand by boosting real wages and profits.

However, another obstacle has arisen: classical political economy does not include the theory of the state in its object of study. The state is regarded as a given. Moreover, the debate among classical economists has remained fixated on the question of the necessary degree of disengagement of the state without raising the issue of its nature. In the analyses of classical economists, there is every indication that the state is regarded as a universal concept with the same meaning everywhere. However, this new form of organisation and exercise of power, which emerged in Western Europe from the seventeenth century onwards, has been shaped differently, particularly in Third World countries following the decolonisation movement. An analysis of the nature of the state and its relationship with the economy is therefore a prerequisite for any consideration of the issues involved in the transition from an extractive and rentier economy to a productive one.

The other choice is that of an analysis based on the State theory, a constitutive category of political science par excellence. Nevertheless, another problem arises, which is that of the interpretative capacities of a single category of social science for a global social phenomenon such as rent. This phenomenon encompasses not only the nature of the State and its relationship with society, but also the effects of rents on society, and in particular the constitution and reconstitution of the state class, which is not based on productive work but on proximity to the centres that control the distribution of rents. In other words, the emergence, evolution, fragmentations and reconfigurations of these classes controlling the relations of authority within the State are regulated not on the basis of law but by proximity to the political circles as a factor that decides on the allocation of rent. This was not the case at the birth of capitalism and the modern Western State.

On this subject, we would like to make a digression of a methodological nature. It seems to us that the formation of social science disciplines is related to the historical content of the subject studied. Social sciences are concerned with differentiated aspects of social practices in fields, in the sense given to this concept by Bourdieu. The relative indifference of the fields in Algeria makes it impossible to found either a true political economy or a true political science. The first has the market as its object, the latter the State, and these two objects are non-existent in Algeria. Nevertheless, there is wealth in circulation and authority relationships that regulate this circulation. These relationships of authority are totally different from those we know in the context of State regulation in the Western sense. This is what makes it difficult to analyse the phenomenon of rents based solely on the teachings of political economy and political science.

Therefore, within this context, we drew inspiration from the notion of extractivism that emerged in Latin American countries, where capitalism was born under completely different conditions from those in Western Europe. In other words, capitalism was born without the illumination of the Enlightenment. This is exactly the case for an economy like Algeria's.

By highlighting the decisive role of political struggles within and against the powers on the ground, along with the contribution of social movements and environmental issues, extractivism distinguishes itself by combining the questions posed by both political economy and political science. In this respect, the following point should be emphasised: the notions of rents and extractivism are certainly complementary, but they are different.

Rent generally refers to income or profit obtained through ownership of a natural resource or asset, rather than through labour or productive investment. In this case, the oil rent is monopolised and redistributed under the control of the Algerian State according to political criteria. Extractivism, on the other hand, is an economic approach that focuses on the extraction and exploitation of natural resources, often without adequate consideration for the long-term environmental, social or economic impacts. This can take the form of intensive exploitation of natural resources without proper planning for sustainability, depletion of resources, environmental degradation, or exploitation of workers.

Rent can obviously result from extractivism, but not vice versa. In other words, a country can possess abundant natural resources and exploit them sustainably, reinvesting the profits in long-term development initiatives rather than simply benefiting from them as a rent, which is not the case for extractivist countries. This is why we put forward the hypothesis that Algeria is both a rentier and an extractivist country. A close look at the history of the Algerian economy amply demonstrates this. This is the subject of this study.

This study is therefore divided into six chapters.

The first chapter is intended to be introductory, in which we retrace the various reflections on the rentier State, the theories of dependence, Dutch disease and, of course, extractivism. The second chapter is a statistical analysis of the Algerian economy from independence to the present day. It examines the crushing weight of rents in the functioning of the state and society. The third and fourth chapters are devoted to the economic history of Algeria since independence. This is a retrospective analysis of the economic practices of the Algerian State, starting with the design and implementation of the Algerian Development Strategy. This strategy was intended to create a productive economy based on heavy industry. But this failed. We will then analyse the various generations of reforms carried out to remedy the situation, and their results. In other words, we will examine the origins of Algeria's extractive and rentier nature. Finally, the fifth chapter looks at the issue of renewable energy in Algeria. The question is whether this "new" strategy will lead to an alternative economy to the current rentier and extractive one, or whether, on the contrary, it will reinforce the rentier nature of the economy by diversifying it.

We will end with a number of summary remarks that serve as a general conclusion.

1 Extractivism, the resource curse and the vicissitudes of the rentier state

Introductory thoughts

1.1 Introduction

Extractivism is a term that comes from the Portuguese "*Extractivismo*" The notion relates to "*a mode of capitalist accumulation that is structured with the colonial empires, and is based on the massive exploitation of raw materials to the metropolises,*" states Alberto Acosta (2015). Moreover, according to the author, extractivism as a particular mode of accumulation began to develop on a massive scale around 500 years ago (with the conquest of America, Africa and Asia). It is clear that the concept has been enriched to such an extent that it has become a polysemous notion over time. This is because the concept covers a wide range of situations. It refers not only to the intensive exploitation of minerals and oil, but also to agriculture, forestry, etc., in short, to everything related to the intensive exploitation of the earth's resources and the biosphere. The concept of extractivism also has another distinctive feature. It is not limited to the phenomena of extraction or to the way in which this is carried out, but to the use of the revenues generated by this exploitation. This approach requires us to reflect on the question of power and the internal and external balance of power in the sharing of the benefits of extractivism.

Extractivism is an old but ever-growing phenomenon. Initially focused on raw materials, extractivism now affects all non-renewable natural resources. It generates colossal revenues on which entire societies depend. These revenues, which are external to the local economy, are clearly not generated by investment, productive work, innovation and so on. They are the result of the exploitation of nature. Consequently, they are not distributed according to the place and class that emerges through work. They are generally provided in a discretionary manner on the basis of political criteria for clientelistic purposes. Extractivism is also characterised by dependence on the international market and repetitive and sometimes violent price fluctuations, which make extractive economies vulnerable and prone to recurrent crises.

As an object of study, extractivism covers disparate political, economic and sociological realities. It covers developed countries as well as less developed ones, and the market realities of both Northern and Southern economies.

DOI: 10.4324/9781003665571-2

In this respect, it should be pointed out that not all extractive economies are necessarily rentier, as in the case of Canada, Norway, the United States, Russia and Indonesia. In addition, there are economies that are rentier but not extractivist, such as countries that have benefited from foreign aid and/or royalties linked to trade routes, like Palestine or Egypt. In other words, rents in the broad sense do not necessarily come from extractive activities. On the other hand, we can safely say that the majority of Third World countries are part of the International Division of Labour through activities that generate rents.

There are many different ways of deciphering the dysfunctions from which extractivist economies suffer. First, there is that of rents and the vicissitudes of the rentier state, then that of the curse of natural resources explained by the theory of Dutch disease and Institutional Economics and finally extractivism, which encompasses the previous theories.

1.2 Annuities and the vicissitudes of the rentier state

It should be remembered that, at its inception, the aim of classical political economy was to identify and combat rents and the drain on production that they provoked. The aim was to liberate the dynamics of accumulation by disqualifying the predatory social classes, whose continuity is ensured by the political context favoured by the rentier logic. In this sense, it is no exaggeration to say that political economy was born with the aim of extinguishing rents and delegitimising the income of the social strata that appropriate them in order to free up the surplus product created by the exploitation of labour power.

The purpose of political economy is to analyse the processes by which wealth is created and distributed. It is a rational conceptualisation of the flows of material wealth created by labour and distributed among the members of civil society according to the price mechanism, the formation of which obeys the logic of supply and demand.

Like other social sciences, its object is both historical and critical: historical, because it is marked by the context of its birth, and critical because it seeks not only to describe how things work, but also and above all to discover the conditions for freeing the dynamics of accumulation and the optimal ways of distributing wealth in order to ensure the infinite continuity of the development process.

At the birth of political economy, the opposition was between the emerging capitalist mode of production and the reigning but dying feudal order. It should be remembered that the object of political economy is based on two main ideas: labour is the only source of wealth (A. Smith) and rent is an economically illegitimate income (D. Ricardo).

The seminal works of the two pioneers of political economy, A. Smith and D. Ricardo, were aimed at both destroying the feudal order and establishing (or strengthening) the liberal order, which was considered the only way to lift humanity out of underdevelopment and the arbitrary rule of feudal rentiers. Their aim was to discover the factors that prevent economies from following the dynamics of accumulation, and the laws that allow economic rationality to permeate the relations of production and distribution. The results of these studies are indisputable: economic development can only be achieved through the relentless struggle to extinguish rents and rentier positions and by rehabilitating the value of work and placing it at the heart of society's concerns.

Historically, the first form of rent identified was land rent. This is held by landowners. It is the price of renting their land to farmers. It was first paid in labour time, then in kind, before it became pecuniary. In the early days of the feudal system, peasants devoted part of their working time to cultivating the land of the landowner and the rest to working on "their" small plot of land loaned by the landowner. This form of land rent payment developed into a payment in kind, meaning that the farmer would devote all his time to working the landowner's land and at the end of the harvest, he would hand over part of the produce to the landowner. The rent was therefore paid in proportion to the total production.[1]

When the agricultural economy was predominant, the payment of rents was socially legitimised because land was seen as a source of wealth. The physiocratic view that non-agricultural activities were sterile fits into this context. For the physiocrats, wealth came from the bounty of the land, so the net product had to be captured by the productive class, in this case, landowners. The theoretical justification for this view stems from the observation that the value of agricultural products is far greater than the means employed in the production process. The difference, therefore, naturally accrues to the owners of the land.

However, with the development of capitalism, particularly agrarian capitalism, which marked the end of the feudal monopoly on land, new conceptions of rent emerged. First, that of A. Smith (1776), who linked rent to the existence of a monopoly, and then that of D. Ricardo, who delegitimised rent by considering that the interests of landowners ran counter to the interests of the community: "*The rent of land, considered as the price paid for the use of land, is therefore naturally a price of monopoly,*" (*asserts* A. Smith, and "the interests of landlords are always opposed to the interests of the community." Smith, and "*the interest of landlords is always opposed to the interest of all other classes in the community,*" Ricardo goes on to say (1997, p. 552). Ricardo went further, advocating the nationalisation of land in order to abolish land rent, the development of which was causing a downward trend in profits, leading capitalism towards a stationary state.

Later works by classical theorists did not depart from this rule of opposing rent to the development of the productive economy. However, the concept of rent is not confined to its historical form, which is land rent. It was generalised to all forms of monopoly that block competition and prevent the formation of equilibrium prices considered to be natural, since they result from the fundamental law of supply and demand.

Income from the sale of raw materials on the international market, in general, is a form of rent. It comes from the difference between the price at which they are sold and the production costs of subsoil products. It is a gift of nature that is monopolised by the State on behalf of the community. The resulting rent is not a new creation of value; it is a transfer that can have as negative an impact on wages and profits as land rent. Worse still, rent has even more perverse effects because it is external to the local labour process. It gives rise to the rentier State, which monopolises its use. As a result, it becomes autonomous from society and falls prey to political powers that privatise it, giving rise to the phenomena of corruption, clientelism and predation.

Thus, the oil rent monopolised by the State, which injects part of it to maintain its clientele among workers in the form of wages and other subsidies without any productive counterpart, gives rise to a number of economic and socio-political phenomena which feed off each other to create a situation in which neither wage levels nor profit rates can be high enough to trigger a dynamic of accumulation.

At the economic level, the injection of money (the oil rent) without any productive counterpart causes inflation. In addition to throwing the price system and the optimal allocation of resources out of balance, inflation erodes purchasing power, particularly of fixed incomes, and reduces effective demand and the propensity to save. When real wages fall, workers retaliate by demanding higher nominal wages, which in turn reduces profits. In addition, the reduction in national savings makes investment more expensive and makes the entire economy dependent on public investment alone, which has repercussions for employment and wages. It is a vicious circle that is constantly fuelling itself, leading to the devaluation of the value of work and the spread of rentier behaviour at all social levels.

At the socio-political level, the perverse effects of rents are as diverse as they are numerous. Rent allows the political regime to become autonomous from society, enabling it to exert a relationship of domination over its members, thus preventing the formation of autonomous spaces likely to give rise to an economic society reproducing itself through work. As a result, rents provoke profound changes in favour of the idle social strata whose reproduction is based on the capture of speculative rents. We are thus witnessing the emergence of an accelerated process of transformation of political power into market assets. In this case, the state is taken over by vast networks of clientele whose accumulation of wealth is based on "illegal" enrichment combining corruption, fraudulent practices and the development of the informal market (Ouchichi, 2011).

1.3 The natural resource curse thesis

The history of countries richly endowed with natural resources shows the divergent effects of rents on the economic performance of these countries. These resources can provide the basis for a structural transformation of economies, leading them to appreciable levels of economic and social development, as in the case of certain countries such as Norway, Canada, Australia and Botswana, which have succeeded in advancing their development thanks to their natural resources. On the other hand, a growing body of research (Aoune, 2008; Auty, 2001; Bravo-Ortega & De Gregorio, 2005; Brückner, 2010; Sachs & Warner, 1995, 2001) argue that these resources can be an inhibiting factor to economic diversification efforts, leading to negative effects on the structural composition of countries' sectoral productive activities and international trade on the one hand, and slowing down the process of economic emergence on the other. The more concentrated exports are, the more vulnerable they are to external shocks, leading to income volatility and low growth (Agosin & Chanci, 2013). Indeed, the economic performance of most resource-rich countries reveals a counter-intuitive phenomenon in which the use of these resources causes serious distortions in their production systems, reflecting a *natural resource curse* (Auty, 2001; Bravo-Ortega & De Gregorio, 2005; Sachs & Warner, 1995, 2001; Sala-i-Martin, 1997).

1.3.1 Contributions of the natural resource curse theory

As coined by Sachs and Warner in 1995, the *natural resource curse* is defined as the tendency of countries richly endowed with natural resources to lose their competitiveness and where the perception of corruption is abused. This resource can lead to under-investment in domestic human capital and a decline in the competitiveness of other economic sectors, which can ultimately affect the growth prospects of the nation that is supposed to benefit from the resource wealth.

The export of resources, therefore, appears to be much more detrimental to economic growth than their scarcity. This is the *paradox of abundance*, or the *curse of natural resources*.

Since the pioneering work of Gelb (1984), Auty (1993) and Sachs and Warner (1995), the term *Natural Resource Curse has* been used to describe the poor performance of resource-rich countries. Sachs and Warner highlighted the existence of a statistically significant negative relationship between the share of primary exports in gross domestic product or total exports and the growth rate. This led to a large body of theoretical and empirical work examining the paradox of plenty. Some have focused on whether or not the curse exists (Auty, 1993, 2001; Sachs & Warner, 1995, 2001). Others have sought to understand and explain the various mechanisms by which natural resources hold back economic development in countries that are richly endowed with

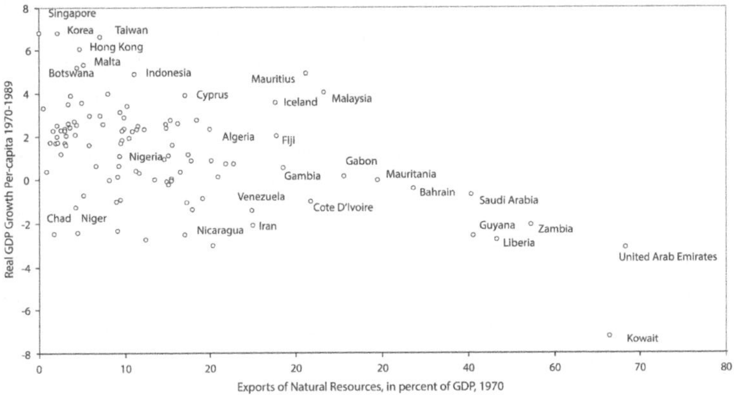

Figure 1.1 Growth and natural resources 1970–1989. Photograph by Sachs and Warner (2001, p. 829).

them, in other words, how a *blessing* (oil and mining revenues) can turn into a curse (Davis, 1995; Gylfason, 2001; Isham et al., 2003; Khan & Jomo, 2000; Mehlum et al., 2005; Torvik, 2002). Others have tried to find *ways of escaping* the curse, in other words, policies that make it possible to avoid the negative impact of natural resources on economic growth.

For Sachs and Warner, the growth differentials between countries are partly explained by the ratio of exported natural resources to GNP. They found a negative correlation between the ratio of natural resource exports to GNP and real GDP growth over the period 1970–1990. This relationship, presented in the graph by Sachs and Warner (2001), illustrated in Figure 1.1, shows that most of the countries that were rich in natural resources in 1970 did not experience rapid growth in the following years. The *cursed* aspect of natural resources has been argued by several economists through the following mechanisms (Mouhoubi, 2012):

- The loss of comparative advantages in the manufacturing sector. This is the result of the temporary fall in production due to the effects of *learning-by-doing*.
- The decline of the economy through Dutch disease. At the company level, it is the administrations and industrial workers and in particular the owners, who are more alarmist than the economists about their loss of competitiveness following the boom in the mining sector from which the whole economy is benefiting.
- Exposure to price shocks cannot be overcome by mining economies with declining traditional sectors, such as diversified income economies. It is a problem faced by all single-export economies. For Auty (1993, 1994),

the greatest concern is not this aspect of exposure to shocks, but rather the optimistic projections of rents to be reaped and high prices to be maintained in place by the institutions of mining economies. This behaviour is an obstacle to economic diversification and long-term economic growth.

- The excessive optimism of institutions in mining economies about future revenues following price booms leads them to take on large debts against this illusion. When prices depreciate, the costs of the erroneous projections will outweigh the profits already made. Algeria, like many other countries, has experienced this situation.
- Public institutions in mining economies, which hold a large share of mining wealth, intervene in the economy with disproportionate spending. Most of this spending is directed towards social services, which is inconsistent with long-term growth.

1.3.2 Explanatory categories for the natural resource curse

The literature offers several categories of explanation for the curse of natural resources. The first category of explanations is linked to the Dutch disease theory, while the second category looks at explanations linked to institutions and government.

1.3.3 The Dutch disease theory

The explanation for the curse of natural resources is largely based on the theory of Dutch disease, which is essentially characterised by a tendency for the real exchange rate to be overvalued, a decline in the sector exposed to international competition (manufacturing sector), an expansion in the unexposed sector (services sector), and a rise in unit labour costs, induced by the rise in wages. This theory was inspired by the Dutch experience following the discovery and exploitation of natural gas reserves in the Groningen field.

Since the 1970s, the macroeconomic consequences of various external shocks, in particular the two oil shocks of 1973 and 1979, have been analysed using the theory of *Dutch disease*, which explains a paradoxical economic phenomenon in which the abundance of highly lucrative natural resources coexists with the impoverishment of a large part of the population (Ghizlain, 2013). The consequences of this phenomenon on economic performance are pernicious and affect the main determinants of economic growth, such as investment, savings and education. The aim of this theory was therefore to show how the discovery of a natural resource can, in the long term, be impoverishing for a country.

Alongside the notion of *Dutch disease*, highlighted in the case of the Dutch economy, other so-called *Booming Sector* models have emerged in Australia. Gregory (1976) discussed the structural changes that occurred in Australia as a result of the development of the mining sector. He explained that this was followed by a relative decline in the mining industry. The second oil crisis of 1979–1980 revived interest in the *Dutch disease* theory, which has been the subject of an abundant theoretical literature (Bruno & Sachs, 1982; Corden, 1984; Corden & Neary, 1982; Neary & van Wijnbergen, 1986; Van Wijnbergen, 1984). Oil exploitation in the United Kingdom, Nigeria and Norway, and mineral exploitation in Australia, have had similar effects to those observed in the Netherlands (Gregory, 1976).

Since the 1990s, another current of theory has elucidated the *theory of the curse of natural resources*. This current is in line with the political economy approach to explaining long-term growth. A country's institutions and constitutional system are key elements in the management of natural resources and condition the negative effect they can have on growth (Anderson & Aslaksen, 2008; Mehlum et al., 2006). In this respect, Dutch disease is not inevitable. Far from being determined by structure, the extent to which a country suffers from Dutch disease depends on the choice of policies adopted.

1.3.4 Institutional economics and its new version included

Unquestionably, one of the most spectacular advances in economic science in recent decades has been the recognition of the imperative need to take account of the role of institutions in understanding economic phenomena. Indeed, under the impetus of leading authors such as North (1990), Baumol (1996), Hall and Jones (1999) and Easterly (2006), an institutionalist turn has taken place in economics. It was in the United States that neo-institutionalism developed in the 1980s to become the "*new mainstream*" and the authority in economic research.

In fact, awareness of the importance of institutions is hardly new and dates back to the very birth of political economy. Nevertheless, it should be noted that the term "institutionalist" was used for the first time by W. Hamilton in 1918 at a conference of the *American Economic Association (AEA)*, regarded as the founding moment of institutionalist economics and the group of researchers who led it as the founders of the approach nicknamed "old institutionalism." Thus, after the long wandering caused by neo-classical deviance and its variants, political economy is returning to its epistemological originality. The founders of political economy sought to understand the process by which wealth is created and distributed, and to discover the laws that cause and govern the dynamics of accumulation.

It is generally accepted that one of the distinctive features of institutional analysis is that it is not rooted in a single theoretical approach. Instead, it combines ideas from several paradigms while integrating the institutional dimension into economic facts. It is, as Chavance (2007) defines it, "*a family of theories that share the thesis that institutions count in the study of economics, that they constitute an essential object of reflection*" (p. 3). As it happens, it is above all the neo-institutionalist movement, led by D. North, that has produced an elaborate theory of economic development linked to institutions.

Indeed, after many years of deliberately ignoring all sorts of extra-economic foundations of the economy as knowledge by the marginalists, the neo-institutionalist current developed a synthesis between the analysis of institutions and neoclassical thought, in response to the growing difficulties raised by the new context of global economic crisis and the problem of underdevelopment. The analytical impasses faced by mainstream economic thought in the 1970s, in the light of the economic crisis that plagued the developed economies during that decade, and the persistence of underdevelopment despite a multitude of strategies being implemented in supposedly developing countries, have led to the re-emergence of the so-called institutional school of economic thought and analysis, whose originality lies in its consideration of institutions in the understanding of economic issues and facts. This reorientation of economic issues led, a few years later, to the affirmation of the current of institutional analysis in economics, particularly from the 1990s onwards.

The literature on institutional economics maintains that a nation's economic performance depends on the quality of its institutions[2] (Acemoglu & Robinson, 2012; Acemoglu et al., 2004; North, 1990). Good institutions (inclusive institutions) are those with the capacity to encourage economic agents to undertake and innovate, to guarantee trust and freedom and to converge private objectives with social objectives. So underdevelopment is all about extractive institutions. These are structured in such a way as to extract resources from the majority by the minority (*the insiders*), far from guaranteeing property rights or providing incentives for economic activity. They reward rent-seeking behaviour, aimed at diverting gains from productive activity to non-productive agents. In the latter case, productive efficiency is lower, and the dynamics of accumulation come to a standstill.

Daron Acemoglu and James Robinson (2012) answer the fundamental question "*why do some nations succeed while so many others fail?*" by highlighting the close link between political and economic institutions: the economy depends on politics; the quality of economic institutions depends on the quality of political institutions. The question of political power (de jure and/or de facto) is central. While de facto (informal) political power influences, or even determines, the way in which existing de jure political institutions (*formal political institutions*) operate, the latter affect the choice of economic institutions. In turn, convergence towards inclusive economic institutions without the convergence of political institutions (Figure 1.1) can only be an ephemeral measure, with an uncertain future (Acemoglu & Robinson, 2019).

For these authors, countries prosper when they develop political and economic institutions based on inclusion, and fail when these are in the hands of oligarchies bent on enriching themselves at the expense of their populations.

For Shirley (2003), good institutions are those that promote economic development, i.e., those that encourage trade (by reducing transaction costs and improving trust) and those that encourage the state to respect private property. Philippot (2009) proposed a detailed analysis of the channels through which natural resources affect institutions. His aim to go beyond the analysis in terms of corruption and predatory behaviour that is often favoured by authors. He detailed other mechanisms, such as civil wars, poor economic policy decisions, authoritarian regimes and the inability to invest in institutions because of weak tax systems. His results show that, whatever the institutional indicator used, countries abundantly endowed with natural resources are characterised by poorer institutional quality.

Natural resource endowment is associated with higher levels of corruption, poorer regulation, greater political instability and less developed civil and political liberties. This negative effect is even more pronounced for concentrated resources and for oil and gas revenues (Sala-i-Martin & Subramanian, 2003; Isham et al., 2005). On the other hand, diffuse resources do not seem to have a negative effect on institutional quality. They may even have a positive effect, which is in line with Engerman and Sokoloff (2002). Torvik (2001) has empirically demonstrated that an abundance of natural resources leads to an increase in *rent-seeking* behaviour and a decrease in income. The author conceives of an economy with four sectors:

- Natural resources sector producing R units without inputs.
- A production sector that produces on the basis of a constant return to scale, where one unit of labour is required to produce one unit of goods.
- Modern production sector that produces with increasing returns to scale, where production requires a unit of contractors and "F" of labour.
- Rent-seekers, who are entrepreneurs who engage in rent-seeking, through political competition or corruption in order to redistribute income in their favour.

It assumes an economy without foreign trade, so that there is no rent from international trade, and in order to focus on the impact of rent from natural resources. It also assumes that the tax rate is constant and that natural resources do not modify the composition of production. Using his model, Torvik (2001) concluded that there is a negative effect of the abundance of natural resources, which encourages entrepreneurs to focus on an unproductive activity, i.e., rent-seeking, to the detriment of a productive sector that has become less profitable in the presence of these resources. The reduction in the number of production firms is synonymous with a reduction in wages to be paid and, therefore, an increase in unemployment rates, thus affecting the quality of social well-being.

For Atkinson and Hamilton (2003), the curse reflects the government's inability to manage the large revenues from natural resources. These revenues are at the root of the persistence of inadequate government policies. Indeed, both authors note that countries richly endowed with natural resources have, on average, a negative real savings rate, unlike resource-poor countries. Moreover, public investment is insignificant. However, when interacting with the rent variable, this variable becomes positively significant, showing that well-endowed countries with a higher rate of public investment have grown faster.

For Subramanian and Sala-i-Martin (2003), controlling the institutional environment makes it possible to avoid the direct negative effect of natural resources on growth. Papyrakis and Gerlagh (2004) empirically tested the impact of natural resources on corruption, investment, openness to the outside world, terms of trade and education. They conclude that the wealth of natural resources is a growth factor provided that indirect negative effects are excluded. On the other hand, if transmission channels are included, the overall effect of natural resources on economic growth is strongly negative. Papyrakis and Gerlagh (2006) have identified three channels through which natural resource wealth affects economic growth. Firstly, natural resources lead to a deterioration in the quality of institutions through rent-seeking. Secondly, they contribute to a deterioration in external trade conditions, as well as reducing investment in high-level education.

Mehlum et al. (2006) have shown that the quality of institutions determines whether the elites in place in a country will appropriate wealth or use it productively. They also found that *rent-seeking* behaviour and poor institutional quality are as prevalent in democratic as in autocratic regimes.

Isham et al. (2003), using indicators that measure the quality of institutions, demonstrate the negative aspect of natural resources on economic growth while introducing the endogeneity of institutions with natural resources as explanatory factors. Their results suggest that the effect of natural resources on economic performance and the quality of institutions depends on the nature of the primary products taken into consideration, while highlighting a more harmful effect of *concentrated* resources than diffuse crops.

Belarbi et al. (2015) in turn assessed the interaction effect between resource dependence and institutional quality using a panel model over the period from 1996 to 2009, covering 23 oil-producing countries. The results show that in industrialised countries, institutional quality reduces the effect of resources on growth, whereas in countries such as Algeria, this mechanism does not operate.

1.4 Extractivism, its typology and pathologies

The issue of the extraction of natural resources is increasingly addressed through the concept of extractivism, characterised as a development model based on the extraction and export of raw materials, whether minerals and fossil fuels (oil, gas, coal, silver, gold, etc.) or agricultural and forestry products grown in monocultures (African palm, soya, sugar cane, etc.). Such activities belong to the primary sector of the economy and do not create added value.

1.4.1 Concept of extractivism

Gudynas (2009) defines the notion of extractivism as a method of extracting natural resources, in large amounts and at intense rates, primarily for export as raw materials with little or no processing. Therefore, extractivism involves a dual process: extracting a natural resource from the ground and exporting the resource outside the producing country. The dynamism of the economy is thus based on this extraction/export duality.

In a way, this is a continuation of the promotion of export-led growth, which, in the 1980s and 1990s, encouraged countries to specialise in a sector of the economy considered to be their comparative advantage, such as basic manufacturing or textiles. Export-led growth was achieved without regard for the development of an industrial structure that would enable the economy to diversify and substitute for imports. Extractivism simplifies this approach even further as it does not consider the development of a national industry and limits itself to identifying that which sells most expensively on international markets before it is extracted (Tremblay Pepin & Hébert, 2013).

The concept of "extractivism" has two important elements (Randriamaro, 2018):

- The first element relates to the process of extracting raw materials such as minerals, oil and gas, as well as water, fish and forest products, and even new forms of energy such as hydroelectricity and forms of industrial agriculture, which often involve land and water taken over by the extractive industries.
- The second element concerns the conditions under which the extraction process takes place and the interests it serves, within the framework of a dominant and highly unequal development model geared towards exploiting and marketing the natural resources of the South for export to the rich economies of the North. Exactivism has often created relationships of dependence and domination between suppliers and consumers of raw materials.

Extractivism is an ancient phenomenon that has existed since colonial times, and the term has strong historical and symbolic significance. Its impact has been felt mainly in Latin America, but also in Africa and Asia, during colonisation, when capitalism was always dependent on extractive economic activities (Galeano, 1971). Colonial extraction provided the colonialists with raw materials, energy and cheap food to help them develop and accumulate capital. Colonialism was a structural instrument for the appropriation and unequal consumption of the world's resources. The methods of extraction during the colonial era had a huge social, economic and environmental impact. Extractivism also had a huge negative impact on the environment and, therefore, on the livelihoods of local people.

Extractivism may be ancient, but it remains a topical phenomenon. The economies of developed countries are based on growth, which means there is a huge demand for natural resources. What is more, emerging countries such as China, Brazil and India are expressing a major need for raw materials for their development. This is why the resource-rich countries of Latin America have focused on extracting and exporting natural resources.

1.4.2 Typology of extractivism according to Eduardo Gudynas (1971)

Gudynas (2010) has distinguished three types of extractivism:

1.4.2.1 Predatory extractivism

This form of extractivism is currently dominant in Africa and other parts of the world. It has serious social, environmental, economic and political impacts. This category includes neo-extractivism, which has seen efforts by some progressive and/or socialist States in Latin America and Africa to strengthen the role of the State in the exploitation and appropriation of natural resources in recent years (Gudynas, 2010; Aguilar, 2012). To this end, laws and policies have been established to ensure national redistribution through the provision of public and social services. These services are financed directly by the profits generated by the extraction of natural resources by governments.

However, according to some analysts, Latin American neo-extractivism has demonstrated the limits of this model of expecting exports and foreign investment to solve historical and structural problems of inequality, inequity and, above all, environmental destruction (Aguilar, 2012, p. 7). As such, in this new model of development, extractivism is reinforced by governments, leading to more conflict over natural resources and increased externalisation of social and environmental costs to communities, without meaningful employment opportunities or better living conditions in these affected communities (Randriamaro, 2018).

1.4.2.2 Cautious or moderate extractivism

This type of extractivism takes into account certain social and environmental standards (which are still contested), but which nevertheless serve as the economic basis for a country or region, as well as a certain degree of community participation. Nevertheless, this form of extractivism does not substantially alter the current structure of accumulation and does not move away from the predatory appropriation of nature.

1.4.2.3 Essential extraction

This form is not a model of extractivism, as it refers to reduced resource extraction. Its main objective is to extract as little as possible; to promote sustainability through recycling; to strengthen laws, policies and regulatory systems to eliminate inequitable flows of materials and resources, to put an end to the pressure on ecosystems, to minimise greenhouse gas emissions, and so on.

1.4.3 Some pathologies of extractivism

The history of the region shows that the extractivist process has led to widespread poverty, encouraged recurrent economic crises and, at the same time, generalised a rentier state mentality. All these factors have weakened democratic institutions, encouraged corruption, de-structured local societies and communities and seriously damaged the environment. The situation is further complicated by clientelist and patrimonial practices, which contribute to slowing down the construction of citizenship (Acosta, 2015).

In addition, the abundance of natural wealth that characterises first-exporting economies tends to alter the economic structure and the allocation of factors of production. It also leads to a regression in terms of redistribution, associated with a greater concentration of wealth. This explains why extractive countries have not been able to take full advantage of the gains resulting from global economic growth and technical progress, especially as these countries often do not themselves process raw materials.

Extractivist economies are also characterised by the structural heterogeneity of their production systems, in other words, the coexistence of high-productivity production systems with other, more archaic, subsistence systems, as well as a disarticulation of economic structures. These are marked by an important focus of exports on a few primary products, the non-existence of sufficiently dense horizontal diversification in industry, weak complementarity between the different sectors of the economy and a virtual absence of vertical integration. This type of extractivist economy often functions according to an enclave logic and a productive apparatus tied to the vicissitudes of the global market (Acosta, 2015).

The concept of extractivism is not restricted to conservative governments adopting neoliberal policies. It also applies to the progressive left-wing or centre-left governments that successively came to power in most Latin American countries during the 2000s, and which promoted a desire for social transformation with a more active role for the State in reducing inequality and fighting poverty. The concept of "neo-extractivism" has thus replaced that of extractivism, referring to policies that strengthen the role of the state in the exploitation and ownership of resources, which is a development that has gained ground around the world.

Nevertheless, for Gudynas and Acosta, extractivism and neo-extractivism are just two sides of the same curse (Acosta, 2015). While neo-extractivism is the hallmark of policies adopted by socialist governments for the equitable redistribution of wealth, the country's economic structure is not thought through any differently and remains entirely dependent on international markets. As a result, the economies concerned remain weak and technologically dependent on multinational firms (Duc, 2017).

Notes

1 This is the logic behind the khemassat, which was highly developed in Algeria under French colonisation. Under this system, the farmer is entitled to 1/5 of the total production, hence the name khemassat (one fifth in Arabic), with the rest going to the landowner.

2 Institutions are defined in relation to different levels. Douglas North (1991) uses this very broad concept to designate all the formal rules (laws and regulations) dictated by the state and the informal rules (culture, customs, etc.) that govern human interaction. For more information, see: Douglas North (1991), Institutions. Journal of economic perspectives, Vol. 5, No. 1, winter 1991, pp. 97–112.

References

Acemoglu, D., Johnson, S., & Robinson, J. A. (2004). Institutions as the fundamental cause of long-run growth. In P. Aghion & S. Durlauf (Eds.), Handbook of Economic Growth (pp. 385–472). Amsterdam: Elsevier.

Acemoglu, D., & Robinson, J. A. (2012). Why nations fail: The origins of power, prosperity, and poverty. New York: Crown Business.

Acemoglu, D., & Robinson, J. A. (2019). The narrow corridor: States, societies, and the fate of liberty. New York: Penguin Press.

Acosta, A. (2015). L'extractivisme et ses pathologies. La lutte pour la survie et la justice climatique en Afrique du Nord. Ritimo. https://www.ritimo.org/L-extractivisme-et-ses-pathologies

Agosin, M. R., & Chanci, M. (2013). Export diversification dynamics in Latin America (MPRA Paper No. 44241). University Library of Munich.

Aguilar, C. (2012). *Transitions towards post-extractivist societies in Latin America: an answer to the EU Raw Materials Initiative*. Dublin Ireland: Southern Alternatives Policy Report.

Anderson, G., & Aslaksen, S. (2008). Constitutions and the resource curse. Journal of Development Economics, 87(2), 227–246.

Aoune, S. C. (2008). La rente pétrolière et le développement économique dans les pays exportateurs [Doctoral dissertation, Université Paris Dauphine].

Atkinson, G., & Hamilton, K. (2003). Savings, growth and the resource curse hypothesis. World Development, 31(11), 1793–1807.

Auty, R. M. (1993). Sustaining development in mineral economies: The resource curse thesis. London: Routledge.

Auty, R. M. (1994). The resource curse thesis: Minerals in Bolivian development, 1970–90. Singapore Journal of Tropical Geography, 15(2), 95–111. https://doi.org/10.1111/j.1467-9493.1994.tb00055.x

Auty, R. M. (2001). Resource abundance and economic development. Oxford: Oxford University Press.

Baumol, W. J. (1996). Entrepreneurship: Productive, unproductive, and destructive. Journal of Business Venturing, 11(1), 3–22. https://doi.org/10.1016/0883-9026(94)00014-X

Belarbi, Y., Sami, L., & Souam, S. (2015). Effects of institutions and natural resources in a multiple growth regime (Working Paper No. 905). Economic Research Forum. https://econpapers.repec.org/RePEc:erg:wpaper: 905.

Bravo-Ortega, C., & De Gregorio, J. (2005). The relative richness of the poor? Natural resources, human capital and economic growth (Policy Research Working Paper No. 3484). World Bank. https://hdl.handle.net/10986/8923.

Brückner, M. (2010). Natural resource dependence, non-tradables, and economic growth. Journal of Comparative Economics, 38(4), 461–471.

Bruno, M., & Sachs, J. D. (1982). Input price shocks and the slowdown in economic growth: The case of U.K. manufacturing. Review of Economic Studies, 49(5), 679–705.

Chavance, B. (2007). L'économie institutionnelle. Paris: La Découverte.

Corden, W. M. (1984). Booming sector and Dutch disease economics: Survey and consolidation. Oxford Economic Papers, 36(3), 359–380.

Corden, W. M., & Neary, J. P. (1982). Booming sector and de-industrialisation in a small open economy. The Economic Journal, 92(368), 825–848.

Davis, G. A. (1995). Learning to love the Dutch disease: Evidence from the mineral economies. World Development, 23(10), 1765–1779.

Duc, T. K. (2017). L'extractivisme sans extraction? Au Groenland, des politiques de développement territorial entre volontarisme minier et dépossessions. Géoconfluences, ENS-Lyon. https://hal.science/hal-01683244

Easterly, W. (2006). The white man's burden: Why the West's efforts to aid the rest have done so much ill and so little good. New York: Penguin Press.

Engerman, S. L., & Sokoloff, K. L. (2002). Factor endowments, institutions, and differential paths of growth among New World economies: A view from economic historians of the United States. In D. Rodrik (Ed.), Institutions and economic performance (pp. 43–66). Princeton University Press.

Farzin, Y. H. (1992). The oil boom and the Dutch disease in a controlled economy: A general equilibrium analysis. World Development, 20(9), 1337–1349.

Galeano, E. (1971). Las venas abiertas de América Latina. México D.F.: Siglo XXI.

Gelb, A. H. (1984). Oil windfalls: Blessing or curse? Oxford: Oxford University Press.

Ghizlain, N. (2013). Maladie hollandaise, un problème d'ajustement : Cas du Congo. *Nap* (8). URL: https://www.thinkingafrica.org/V2/maladie-hollandaise-un-probleme-dajustement-le-cas-du-congo/

Gregory, R. G. (1976). Some implications of the growth of the mineral sector. Australian Journal of Agricultural Economics, 20(2), 71–91.

Gudynas, E. (2009). Diez tesis urgentes sobre el nuevo extractivismo. In O. Lopez & P. Ospina (Eds.), Extractivismo, política y sociedad (pp. 187–225).

Gudynas, E. (2010). Americas Program Report. Washington, DC: Center for International Policy.

Gudynas, E., & Acosta, A. (2015). El buen vivir más allá del desarrollo. In M. Lang & D. Mokrani (Eds.), Más allá del desarrollo (pp. 25–60). Quito: Abya Yala.

Gylfason, T. (2001). Natural resources, education, and economic development. European Economic Review, 45(4–6), 847–859.

Hall, R. E., & Jones, C. I. (1999). Why do some countries produce so much more output per worker than others? The Quarterly Journal of Economics, 114(1), 83–116.

Isham, J., Woolcock, M., Pritchett, L., & Busby, G. (2003). The varieties of resource experience: How natural resource export structures affect the quality of governance (World Bank Policy Research Working Paper No. 2910). World Bank.

Isham, J., Woolcock, M., Pritchett, L., & Busby, G. (2005). The varieties of resource experience: Natural resource export structures and the political economy of economic growth. The World Bank Economic Review, 19(2), 141–174. https://doi.org/10.1093/wber/lhi010

Khan, M., & Jomo, K. S. (2000). Rents, rent-seeking and economic development: Theory and evidence in Asia. Cambridge University Press.

Mehlum, H., Moene, K., & Torvik, R. (2005). Institutions and the resource curse. The Economic Journal, 116(508), 1–20.

Mehlum, H., Moene, K., & Torvik, R. (2006). Cursed by resources or institutions? World Economics, 7(3), 111–125.

Mouhoubi, A. (2012). La gestion de la rente des ressources naturelles épuisables dans la perspective du développement économique: Référence au cas des hydrocarbures en Algérie [Thèse de doctorat en sciences économiques, Université de Béjaïa].

Neary, J. P., & van Wijnbergen, S. (1986). Natural resources and the macroeconomy. Oxford: Basil Blackwell.

North, D. C. (1990). Institutions, institutional change and economic performance. Cambridge: Cambridge University Press.

North, D. (1991), Institutions. *Journal of economic perspectives*, 5(1), 97–112.

Ouchichi, M. (2011). *L'obstacle politique aux réformes économiques en Algérie* [Doctoral dissertation, Université Lyon 2]. HAL Archives Ouvertes. Retrieved from https://shs.hal.science/tel-03596287

Papyrakis, E., & Gerlagh, R. (2004). The resource curse hypothesis and its transmission channels. Journal of Comparative Economics, 32(1), 181–193.

Papyrakis, E., & Gerlagh, R. (2006). Resource abundance and economic growth: A Granger causality analysis. Resource Policy, 31(1), 1–13.

Philippot, C. (2009). Institutions et malédiction des ressources naturelles: enquête sur les voies de dépendance institutionnelle. Revue Tiers Monde, 198, 33–54.

Randriamaro, Z. (2018). L'extractivisme, la féminisation des résistances et les alternatives politiques en Afrique. Alternatives Sud, 25(3), 45–62.

Ricardo, D. (1997/1817). On the principles of political economy and taxation. London: Dent/Dover.

Sachs, J. D., & Warner, A. M. (1995). Natural resource abundance and economic growth (NBER Working Paper No. 5398). National Bureau of Economic Research.

Sachs, J. D., & Warner, A. M. (2001). The curse of natural resources. European Economic Review, 45(4-6), 827–838.

Sala-i-Martin, X. (1997). I just ran two million regressions. The American Economic Review, 87(2), 178–183.
Sala-i-Martin, X., & Subramanian, A. (2003). Addressing the natural resource curse: An illustration from Nigeria. IMF Working Paper No. WP/03/139.
Shirley, M. M. (2003). Institutions and development. In C. Ménard & M. M. Shirley (Eds.). In Handbook of new institutional economics (pp. 611–638). Dordrecht: Springer.
Singer, H. W. (1950). The distribution of gains between investing and borrowing countries. The American Economic Review, 40(2), 473–485.
Smith, A. (1776/2000). Recherche sur la nature et les causes de la richesse des nations (trad. GF-Flammarion). Paris: GF-Flammarion.
Smith, A. (2000). Recherche sur les causes et la nature de la richesse des nations (p. 140). Economica.
Subramanian, A., & Sala-i-Martin, X. (2003). Addressing the natural resource curse: An illustration from Nigeria. IMF Working Paper WP/03/139.
Torvik, R. (2001). Learning by doing and the Dutch disease. European Economic Review, 45(2), 285–306.
Torvik, R. (2002). Natural resource rent, learning and conflict. Journal of Development Economics, 67(2), 455–470.
Tremblay Pepin, S., & Hébert, G. (2013). L'extractivisme et ses alternatives: Approches économiques et politiques. Recherches sociographiques, 54(1), 33–56.
Van Wijnbergen, S. (1984). The "Dutch disease": A disease with a cure? The Economic Journal, 94(376), 41–55.

2 Is Algeria an extractive and rentier country?

Statistics to prove it

2.1 Introduction

In the wake of the global debate on extractivism and the broader literature on rentier states, this chapter puts forward the hypothesis that Algeria represents a hybrid political economy that is simultaneously extractive and rentier. This dual condition is not merely descriptive but structurally significant, reinforcing economic dependency, authoritarian governance and socio-environmental vulnerabilities. Through the combination of statistical evidence and theoretical insights, this chapter explores how the interplay of rentierism and extractivism shapes the Algerian political economy and hinders efforts toward diversification and transformation.

Algeria is one of those countries that are rich in natural resources, which have remained trapped in this structural vulnerability. The structure of its economy is based essentially on oil and gas revenues. Since 1990, oil revenues have accounted for between 30% and 50% of GDP, between 75% and 98% of total exports, and more than 60% of treasury resources have come from oil taxes. What is the country's strength is also its greatest vulnerability. The Algerian economy is exposed to volatile terms of trade. Energy revenues have a major influence on the government's economic policy decisions.

The instability and sudden turnaround in the oil market in recent years remind us of the mid-1980s, when Algeria was plunged into instability and crisis. Already at that time, the negative oil shock of 1986 revealed the extreme vulnerability of the Algerian economy, where rents act as an exogenous variable that determines levels of economic activity, employment and investment, as well as the State's economic policy (Chapter 1 on the disadvantages of extractivism). In the Finance Act, it is the price of oil that determines the state budget, the import programme, the volume of the various subsidies, etc. It also highlights multiple dimensions of the economy: the dysfunctional nature of the production system, which for a long time was masked and overtaken by the importance of oil revenues; the lack of diversification in the supply of goods and services and the rigidity of the structure of exports based on hydrocarbons; and a redistributive economy on which the social compromise that

DOI: 10.4324/9781003665571-3

prevailed in Algeria from the 1970s onwards was built (Dahmani, 2015). The manufacturing sector, which is theoretically a source of long-term growth, accounts for less than 10% of GDP and less than 5% of exports.

Against this backdrop, diversification of the economy has become essential, and is a major challenge that the country must take up very quickly if it is to meet the many economic development challenges it has been facing for several decades. This is one reason why the public authorities have paid particular attention to the development of non-hydrocarbon exports by implementing a number of framework measures designed to promote Algerian production on foreign markets, as well as a number of organisations supporting export activity, particularly non-hydrocarbon exports. However, diversification faces many obstacles, and efforts to launch a real diversification policy have met with mixed results. The country has not been able to undertake a structural transformation of its economy capable of extricating it from this dependence. Indeed, 60 years after independence, and despite several generations of reforms, the country remains fundamentally extractive and rentier.

Algeria exemplifies a political economy that is simultaneously rentier and extractivist in nature, combining the characteristics of both models in a mutually reinforcing dynamic. From a rentier perspective, as defined by Mahdavy (1970) and elaborated by Beblawi and Luciani (1987), the Algerian state relies overwhelmingly on external rents derived from hydrocarbon exports, which have historically accounted for over 90% of export earnings and a substantial portion of public revenues. These rents are monopolised and redistributed by the state, not through mechanisms of productive accumulation, but via clientelist, populist, and centralised governance structures, weakening fiscal accountability and insulating the regime from societal pressures (Elsenhans, 1982; Ouaissa, 2010; Ross, 2001). At the same time, Algeria also conforms to the logic of extractivism, as conceptualised by Latin American scholars such as Gudynas (2009) and Acosta (2013). Its economy is deeply embedded in a model of accumulation based on the large-scale extraction and export of raw natural resources, primarily oil and gas, with minimal domestic processing, limited value-chain integration, and high vulnerability to global commodity price fluctuations. The enclave-like nature of its energy sector—technologically sophisticated yet structurally disconnected from the broader economy—reflects a typical extractivist configuration, which prioritises external demand over endogenous development and often leads to severe territorial, ecological, and social externalities (Brand & Wissen, 2013; Svampa, 2019).

While Algeria has long embodied the characteristics of both a rentier and an extractivist economy, a sharper conceptual differentiation is necessary—particularly in the context of global energy transitions and the rise of so-called green rents.

While rentierism highlights how revenue is politically captured and redistributed, extractivism focuses on the material basis of that revenue and the broader socio-environmental consequences of resource-dependent growth. Algeria's case reveals that these two logics are not mutually exclusive but interdependent: the extractive base generates the rents, and the rentier state reproduces the extractive structure through a combination of subsidised consumption, repression of dissent, and underinvestment in diversification. This dual condition renders Algeria particularly vulnerable to both price shocks and legitimacy crises, as seen in moments of declining oil prices or rising social unrest, and presents significant obstacles to any genuine transition toward a productive or post-extractivist economy.

The recent shift in global energy geopolitics adds a new layer of complexity. As Algeria seeks to position itself within the post-fossil order, the concept of green rents becomes increasingly relevant. Green rents refer to new forms of unearned income derived from renewable energy potential—such as solar radiation, wind corridors, or green hydrogen production—rather than from fossil fuel abundance (Power et al., 2016). While these rents are promoted as instruments of ecological modernisation, they may merely represent a technocratic reconfiguration of existing extractivist and rentier paradigms. Algeria's large-scale renewable energy projects, including solar megaprojects in the Sahara and emerging hydrogen corridors with Europe, remain marked by centralisation, foreign dependency, and the absence of local value-added chains or participatory governance. These initiatives echo what Acosta (2013) has termed "neoextractivism"—a model in which the state, often under the banner of social justice or sustainability, intensifies its control over resource extraction without altering the underlying logic of dependency and dispossession.

Rather than signalling a rupture with the past, Algeria's engagement with green rents risks reproducing the very structural pathologies that have long characterised its rentier-extractivist economy. As Brand and Wissen (2013) argue in their critique of the "imperial mode of living," technocratic environmental governance often fails to address the embeddedness of consumption and production patterns in unequal global power structures. Similarly, Svampa (2019) warns that the extractivist turn toward "green commodities" often generates new conflicts over land, labour and sovereignty, especially in the global South. In Algeria, where industrial policy remains weak, civil society is marginalised, and democratic accountability is fragile, green rents are unlikely to lead to structural transformation in the absence of a clear post-extractivist agenda.

The implications of this continuity are profound. As Acosta (2015) notes, the persistence of extractivism—even in its green or progressive forms—tends to entrench short-termist economic strategies, strengthen patrimonial power relations, and undermine long-term sustainability. Algeria's political economy reflects precisely this dilemma: the illusion of abundant and effortless wealth derived from nature inhibits both democratic accountability and productive investment. Without a radical shift toward inclusive governance, decentralised energy systems, and ecological justice, green rents may simply become another instrument of authoritarian reproduction. In short, Algeria risks falling into what Acosta calls "two sides of the same curse"—the continuity of extractive logic under a new ecological guise.

2.2 The weight of the hydrocarbons sector in Algeria

The production of hydrocarbons (oil and natural gas) in Algeria (estimated at between 30% and 50% of GDP since 1990),[1] is traditionally the cornerstone of the Algerian economy, which continues to grow richer on the back of hydrocarbon export revenues, for these have been the country's main source of rent (between 75% and 98% of exports). The impact of the hydrocarbon sector on public policy is therefore strongly linked to its share of total exports, budget revenues and GDP. The main aim of this section is therefore to highlight the increased dependence of the Algerian economy on energy revenues and to confirm the extractivist and rentier nature of the economy.

2.2.1 Hydrocarbon production and reserves in Algeria

Algeria's subsoil contains large quantities of hydrocarbons, particularly natural gas. Algeria is one of the main suppliers of hydrocarbons to European countries. Total production stagnated for more than a decade before picking up significantly in 2016, but only for natural gas.

2.2.1.1 Oil production

Algeria's crude oil production began in 1957 and grew during the 1960s and 1970s, thanks to the boom in the hydrocarbons sector. Between 1973 and 1979, crude oil production was influenced by the sharp rise in oil prices.

As shown in Figure 2.1, production volumes peaked in 2007 following a sharp increase in global demand for petroleum products. From 2009 onwards, production began to fall, and the situation is now alarming. Algeria produced 1.99 million barrels a day in 2005, compared with 1.47 million in 2022. Algeria is Africa's third-largest oil producer after Libya and Angola. According to a ranking by the specialist portal Trading Economics, Algeria's production of 999,000 barrels a day puts it in the 18th position among the world's biggest oil producers.

2.2.1.2 Natural gas production

Natural gas is an increasingly sought-after raw material, for both environmental and efficiency reasons, particularly for power generation. Production of natural gas began in Algeria in 1961 with the birth of the gas industry at

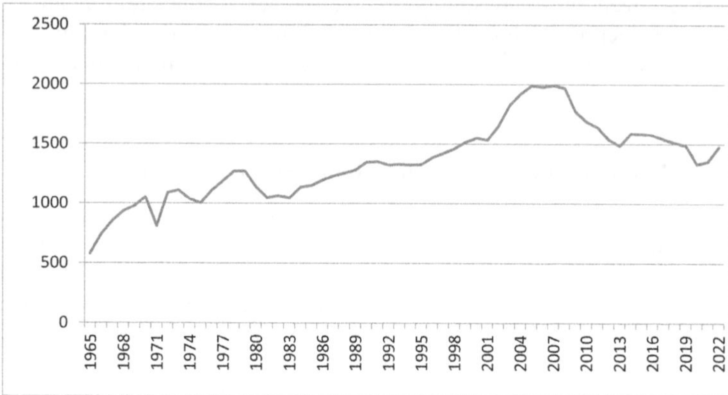

Figure 2.1 Oil production trends in Algeria (1965 to 2022) in trillion cubic metres. Graph created by the author, based on own calculations using data from Statistical Review of World Energy, BP, June 2023.

Hassi R'mel. Initially, production was intended for domestic consumption, but following the increase in global demand for natural gas, Algeria increased its production.

Figure 2.2 shows that between 1980 and 1983, production more than doubled (from 15.4 trillion m^3 to 33.4 trillion m^3). Following the discovery of other gas fields in 1984, Algeria at that time had four gas liquefaction (LNG) complexes with a capacity of 21 million tonnes, making Algeria one of the

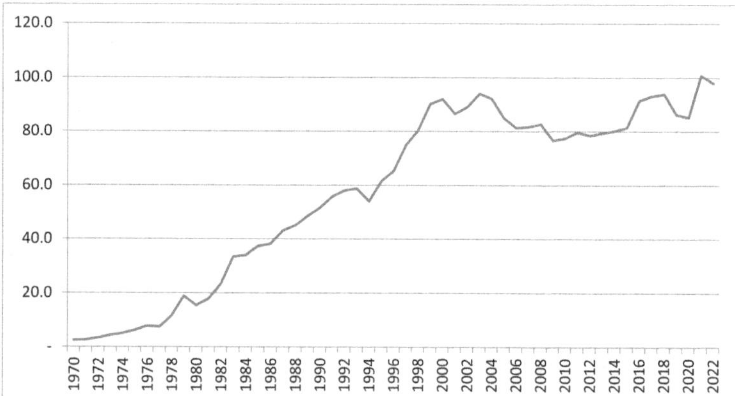

Figure 2.2 Development of natural gas production in Algeria (1970–2022) in trillion cubic metres. Graph created by the author, based on own calculations using data from Statistical Review of World Energy, BP, June 2023.

world's leading LNG producers (particularly during the period from 1998 to 2003), with a production capacity of 93.9 billion tonnes in 2003. It subsequently fell to the second place after Iran in the period 2004–2008, and in the period 2009–2012, it was ranked third in the world. With 91.4 trillion m^3 in 2016, Algeria's gas production represents around 30% of Africa's reserves, 43% of its production and 56% of its exports. Around 60% of Algeria's natural gas production was exported, mainly to the European Union in 2016.[2] Algeria was Africa's leading gas producer that same year, and it will be the world's tenth-largest natural gas producer by 2021.

Proved reserves are those oil and gas resources which, according to available geological and technical information, have a high probability of being recovered in the future.[3] The level of proven reserves can be increased by new discoveries, thanks to exploration activity, the use of new technologies and more favourable economic conditions. They are referred to as P90, because they have a 90% chance of being brought on stream.

2.2.1.3 Proved oil reserves

Algeria is one of the countries with a medium level of proven oil reserves. Most of these are located in the Hassi Messaoud region, the country's largest oil field. According to Sonatrach, around 66% of Algeria remains unexplored or largely underexplored, and the Hassi Messaoud-Dahar province could contain up to 71% of the country's oil reserves of all types (proven, probable, possible).

According to BP estimates (British Petroleum statistics), Algeria's proven oil reserves increased significantly between 1998 and 2004, by around 50%. Since then, they have remained stable at 12.2 billion barrels until 2022, or around 0.7% of the world's reserves (Figure 2.3). These reserves ranked Algeria 17th in the world, and 4th in Africa, behind Libya, Nigeria and Angola.

2.2.1.4 Proved natural gas reserves

Algeria is a gas country rather than an oil one, since proven gas reserves far exceed oil reserves. More than half of the country's proven natural gas reserves are located in the large Hassi R'mel field. The rest of the country's gas comes from gas fields in the southeast. According to BP statistics (British Petroleum statistics), the country's natural gas reserves have been growing steadily since the 1980s.

They have reached record levels since 2002, thanks to access to the most advanced exploration techniques and production facilities. Over the period from 2008 to 2020, the country's natural gas reserves have remained stable, with a capacity of around 4.5 trillion cubic metres per year, or 54 years of production at 2019 rates (Figure 2.4). This places the country 9th in the world (with around 2.4% of the world's reserves), and second in Africa, behind Nigeria.

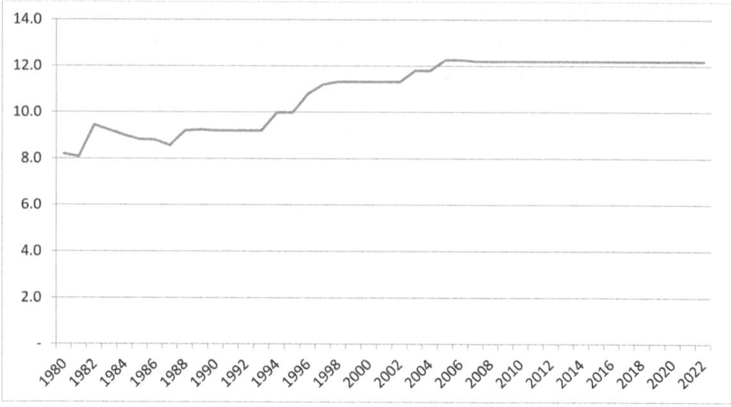

Figure 2.3 Proven oil reserves in Algeria 1980–2022 (billion barrels). Graph created by the author, based on own calculations using data from Statistical Review of World Energy, BP, June 2023.

2.2.2 *The share of hydrocarbon revenues in the main economic indicators*

The production of hydrocarbons in Algeria is traditionally the cornerstone of the Algerian economy, which continues to grow richer by relying on revenues from hydrocarbon exports, which have until now been considered the country's main source of rent (between 75% and 98% of exports). The impact

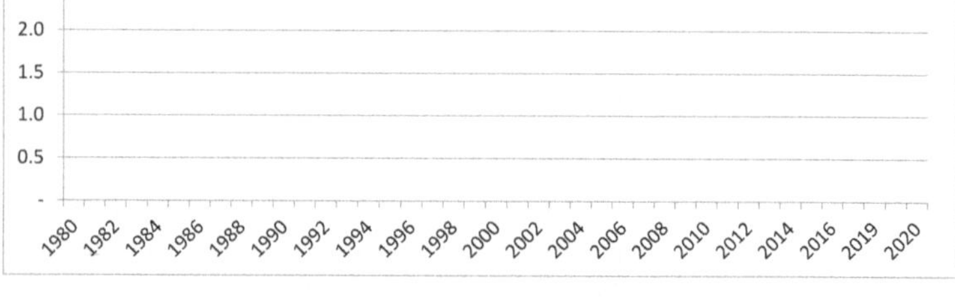

Figure 2.4 Development of proven natural gas reserves in Algeria from 1980 to 2020 (billion cubic metres). Graph created by the author, based on own calculations using data from Statistical Review of World Energy, BP, June 2021.

of the hydrocarbons sector on public policy is therefore closely linked to its share of total exports, budget revenues and GDP. Hydrocarbon exports also predominate in Algeria's total exports.

The Algerian economy is characterised by the clear dominance of hydrocarbons in its exports. The weight of the country's oil and gas exports clearly explains the Algerian economy's dependence on the hydrocarbons sector. Figure 2.5 shows the structure of Algeria's exports over the period 1970–2020.

It is clear from this figure that, for all periods, the share of the hydrocarbons sector dominates Algeria's total exports. During the 1970s, which was a decade marked by the two oil shocks (1973 and 1979), the share of hydrocarbon exports in total exports exceeded an average of 95%. In 1986, despite the counter-oil shock and the drastic fall in hydrocarbon prices, accompanied by a significant drop in foreign currency earnings, the share of hydrocarbon exports in total exports remained dominant and also exceeded the average of 95% during the period 1985–1999.

According to the same figure, hydrocarbon exports dominated the period from 2000 to 2013, with an average of over 97% of total exports. In the second half of 2014, oil prices, expressed in dollars, fell by around 50%. Despite this fall, the share of exports remains dominant and exceeds the average of 94% of total exports.

To sum up, from 1973 onwards, the trend towards specialisation in the export of a single product became more pronounced, and the share of hydrocarbon exports in Algeria's total exports continued to grow, remaining dominant both during periods of favourable international economic conditions and during periods of falling oil and gas prices.

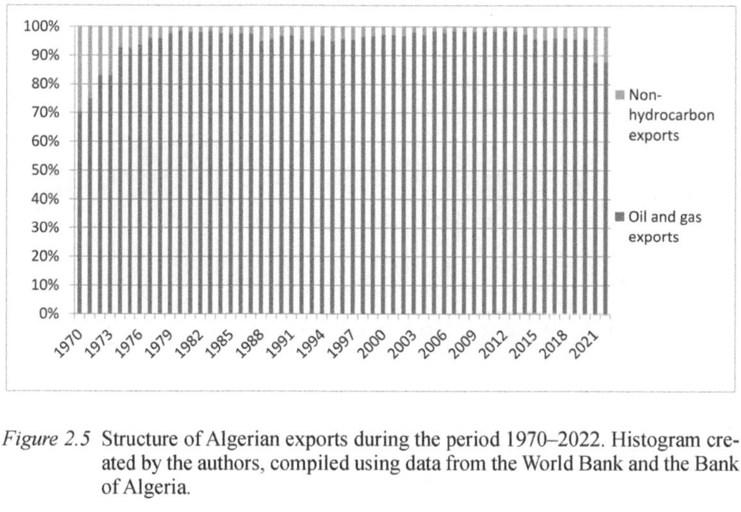

Figure 2.5 Structure of Algerian exports during the period 1970–2022. Histogram created by the authors, compiled using data from the World Bank and the Bank of Algeria.

2.2.2.1 The weight of oil taxation in budget revenue

Revenues from hydrocarbons go to the State via oil taxes. The trend in oil taxation in Algeria logically follows the same trend as the revenue generated by hydrocarbons measured in terms of PPB (price of crude oil). Oil taxation has always acted as a catalyst for the State budget. It is the main budget resource and is closely linked to the price of oil. Since the first oil crisis in 1973–1974, the various Finance Acts have constantly relied on the contribution made by the hydrocarbons sector. Figure 2.6 shows the share of oil revenues in total government budget revenues from 1970 to 2022.

Figure 2.6 shows that just after the first oil shock in 1973, oil taxation accounted for 57.17% of total budget revenue in 1974, compared with 20.93% in 1970. In the period between the two oil shocks of 1973 and 1979, the share of oil taxation exceeded half of budget revenues. This share also increased following the second oil crisis in 1979, reaching 64.35% in 1981. After averaging 55% between 1980 and 1985, the share of oil taxes in total budget revenue fell significantly with the 1986 oil crisis, to 23.9% in 1986 and 22.02% in 1987. This shows the vulnerability of the Algerian economy to negative external shocks in oil prices. Between then and the positive oil price shock in the early 2000s, the average annual share of oil taxes in total government budget revenue was 50.10%. Over the period 2000 to 2007, this share averaged 68.76%, with 74.34% in 2000 and 74.56% in 2006. But with the economic crisis of 2008, oil taxation fell and its share of the State budget reached 44.94% in 2011. By 2022, this share reached 37%.

On average, non-hydrocarbon tax revenues made a small contribution to total State budget resources between 2000 and 2014. Tax revenues from the

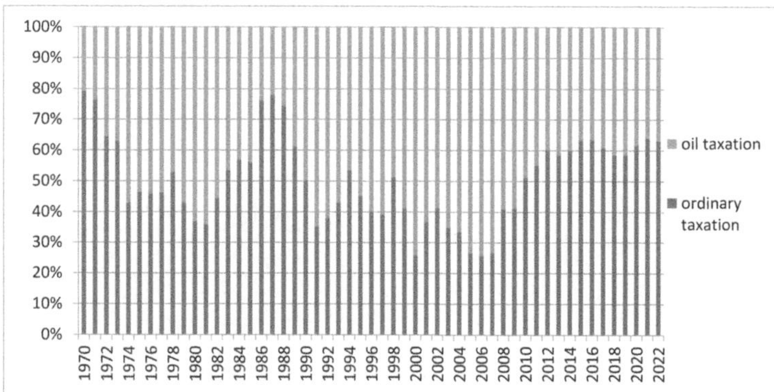

Figure 2.6 Percentage share of oil taxes in total government revenue (1970–2022). Histogram created by the authors, compiled using data from ONS and annual reports of the Bank of Algeria.

hydrocarbons sector, which finance both the State budget and the Revenue Regulation Fund (FRR), represented an annual average of around 70% of total revenues over the same period.

To sum up, oil taxation is the State's main source of revenue (compared with other fiscal resources), which makes public finances vulnerable to sudden falls in oil prices (each negative external and development program is dependent on fluctuations of oil prices). The weight of the hydrocarbons shock leads to a fall in oil taxation and its share of the State budget leaving fiscal policy dependent on oil fluctuations.

2.2.2.2 *The weight of the Oil Sector in GDP*

The low production of tradable goods is one of the problems of extractive and rentier economies. Indeed, several studies have shown that the abundance of rents leads to a decline in the sectors producing these goods. In Algeria, hydrocarbons are the country's main source of income. Revenues from hydrocarbons have made it possible to finance the various economic recovery programmes and considerably reduce the country's external debt.

2.2.2.2.1 SECTORAL CONTRIBUTION TO GROWTH OVER THE PERIOD 1969–1985

A study of the structure of domestic production in Algeria during the period prior to the oil crisis of 1986 highlights the effects of booms in financial resources on the performance of the various sectors of the economy.

Figure 2.7 shows the contribution of the various sectors of economic activity to domestic production in Algeria over the period 1969–1985. It is clear

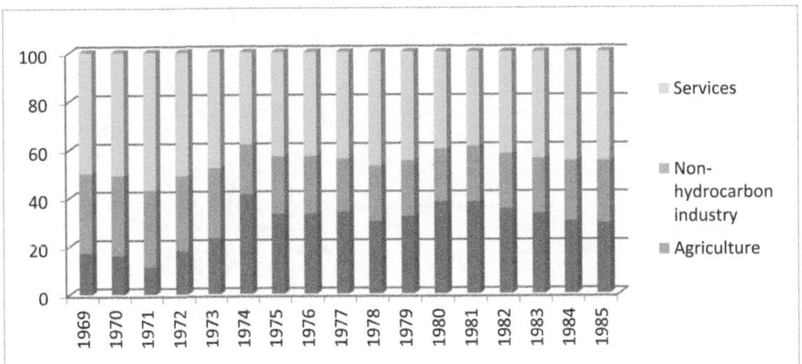

Figure 2.7 Percentage structure of GDP (1969–1985). Histogram created by the author(s), compiled from World Bank data.

from this figure that the hydrocarbon sector's share of domestic production increased considerably following the two oil booms of 1973 to 1974 and 1979 to 1980, reaching 41% and 38% respectively. The non-hydrocarbon sectors, such as agriculture and industry, make only a marginal contribution to GDP. The agricultural sector's share of total GDP fell in 1972 and stabilised at around 10% between 1976 and 1985. The share of the manufacturing sector stabilised at around 18% between 1969 and 1973. This share had fallen since 1974 to 12%. This fall was the result of the increase in the share of the hydrocarbons sector.

As for the services sector, it contributes significantly to GDP. In 1969, its share was 50%, then it fell to 39% in 1981 and rose to 45% in 1984 and 1985. Nevertheless, it is worth noting the increase in the share of the petroleum works sector in order to provide the sector with infrastructure and accompany the booms.

Figure 2.8 shows the structure of trade balances in tradable goods. We can see from this Figure that the trade balances in recorded tradeable goods are all negative except for the two years 1969 and 1970. After experiencing trade surpluses during these two years, the agricultural sector suffered deficits, which became progressively heavier. Exports of agricultural goods have fallen sharply since 1969. Imports, meanwhile, have increased sixfold over the same period (1969–1985). This situation has further aggravated the negative balance of trade in agricultural goods. Developments in trade in manufactured goods have not benefited from the major investments made in the non-hydrocarbon industrial sector, since, in absolute terms, import growth does not match export growth (Mouhoubi, 2012).

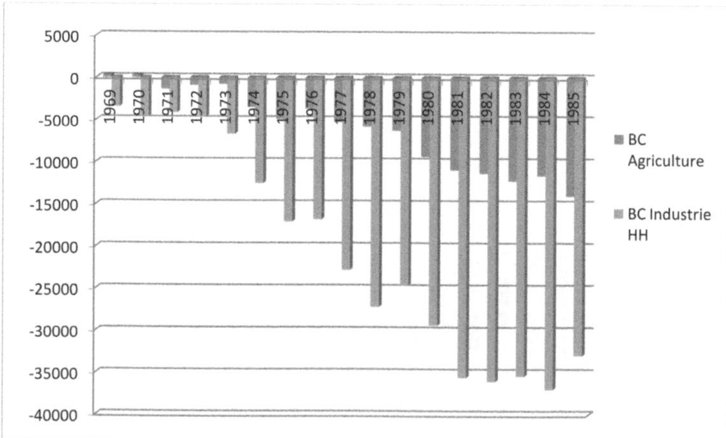

Figure 2.8 Structure of trade balances in tradable goods (1969–1985). Histogram created by the author, compiled from World Bank data.

The explanatory effects of the *Dutch disease*, as highlighted in the first chapter, can be seen in the atrophy of the tradable goods sectors. A boom in the mining sector will produce a surplus in the balance of payments, synonymous with an overall increase in income. If the latter is fully spent, and if the goods in the non-traded sector are not inferior goods, the rise in income will lead to an increase in demand for these goods, which implies a rise in the domestic prices of these goods. The spending effect and the increase in purchasing power have enabled Algerians to consume imported goods at low prices.

Between 1969 and 1985, the Algerian population grew by 70%, while imports increased by 500% and the volume of production fell by 51%. These statistics do not allow us to conclude that, correlatively, the consumption pattern of Algerians has become more luxurious. The increase in recorded imports has boosted the non-tradable goods sector to take over the production factors that have left the tradable goods sector. As a result, after the trade surpluses in the agricultural sector in 1969 and 1970, it is now experiencing deficits that are becoming larger and larger. The significant increase in food imports explains the deterioration in the agricultural situation (Mouhoubi, 2012).

2.2.2.2.2 SECTORAL CONTRIBUTION TO GROWTH BETWEEN 1986 AND 2018

An overview of Figure 2.9 shows that following the 1986 oil crisis, the hydrocarbon sector's share of GDP fell to 14.56% in 1986. This sector represented an average of less than 26% of GDP during the late 1980s and 1990s. The oil

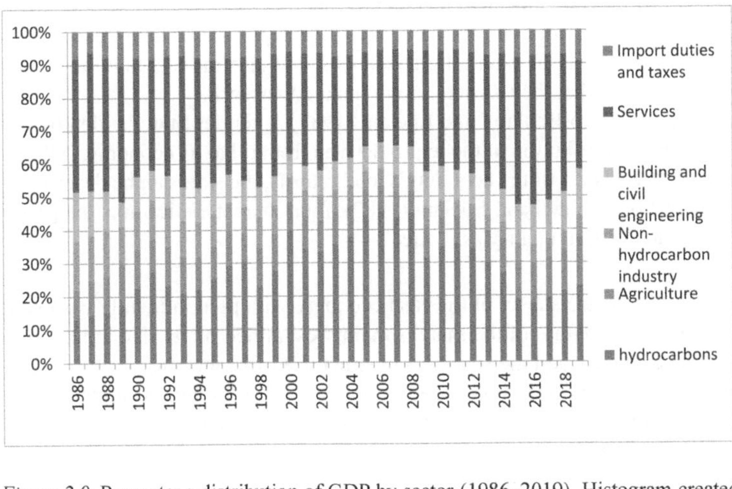

Figure 2.9 Percentage distribution of GDP by sector (1986–2019). Histogram created by the author, based on own calculations using ONS data.

boom of the 2000s has had an impact on the weight of hydrocarbons in the country's national wealth.

From 2000 to 2012, the hydrocarbon sector contributed an average of 38% to GDP, peaking in 2008 at 45.1%, when oil prices reached their highest level. The fall in oil prices in 2014 brought this rate down to 18.8% in 2015. The services sector also plays an important role in the formation of GDP, with an average of over 35% since 2000. The other productive sectors, such as agriculture and industry, make only a marginal contribution to GDP, and their weight in the economy is very low. We can thus see that GDP remains highly dependent on the production behaviour of the hydrocarbons sector, given its weight in GDP formation. It is the country's largest source of wealth, while the contribution of the productive sectors to the economy is minimal and fluctuates from time to time.

2.2.2.3 The extractivist and rentier nature of the Algerian economy and its dependence on natural resource rents

Land rent can be defined as "*income from the gift of nature.*" It is thus generally equated with accrued income from the export of natural resources, particularly oil and gas (Beblawi, 1990). From a political economy perspective, the explanation for the low level of export diversification in resource-rich countries is often based on the theory of the rentier State (Beblawi & Luciani, 2015). This is reinforced by the concept of extractivism, which extends the analysis to the ecological aspects and social consequences of dependence on natural resources.

The rentier nature of an economy can be identified through the weight of the hydrocarbon sector in that economy, and the management of rents by the state. The most common problem faced by export-dependent economies is their vulnerability to external price shocks, and also the fact that they collect colossal rents that their structures are unable to absorb.

According to Beblawi and Luciani (1987), a rentier State is identified by the rate of contribution of the return derived from oil to its economy. If this return exceeds 40% of the economy's total returns, the state can be described as rentier. For Beblawi and Luciani (1987), four characteristics must be present in a State for it to qualify as rentier:

- The State is a subset of the cash economy with predominantly cash situations. The nature of the State is mainly examined by its size in relation to the economy and the sources and structures of its income.
- An economy massively based on income from foreign customers, which therefore does not require a strong national productive sector.
- Only a small proportion of the working population is involved in generating income.
- The government is the main beneficiary of external rent in the economy.

Thus, in a rentier State, national wealth is created by a small fraction of society, unlike an open economy with high levels of foreign trade, which is not considered rentier since the majority of society is actively involved in the wealth creation process. The World Bank, in turn, has adopted the rentier State literature to determine whether a country is a rentier economy through the share of rents in GDP and total exports. Rentier economies are those where at least 10% of GDP and 40% of total exports come from oil activities, making this sector the basis of the economy (Auty, 1993; Nankany, 1979).

To cope with falling oil prices and external revenues, extractive and rentier economies must either maintain the course of hydrocarbon extraction and face major economic reversals (Smith, 1968) or intensify hydrocarbon extraction and accelerate the rate at which deposits dry up in order to maintain living standards (Farzin, 1992). Herb's equation (2005), which measures rentierism, can explain this by assessing the relative importance of rentier incomes.

$$Rentierism = \frac{rentier\ incomes}{sum\ of\ the\ other\ incomes + rentier\ incomes}$$

This ratio tends towards 1 in poor countries where the share of rents in total income is predominant, unlike in industrialised countries with different sources of income. An oil dependency index has been constructed based on the work of Auty (1993), Gelb (1988) and Nankany (1979). It gives the average penetration of oil revenues in a country's three main economic variables. This index, or rentierism, is used to measure a country's oil dependence. It calculates the average share of oil revenues in three economic variables, namely GDP, tax revenues and exports. It provides information on the intensity of the presence of oil revenues in an economy and is calculated as follows:

$$Index\ of\ oil\ dependency = \frac{\left(PIBH/PIB\right) + \left(FP/RT\right) + \left(XH/X\right)}{3}$$

If the oil dependency index tends towards 1, this means that oil revenues tend to predominate in the economy. If the index tends towards 0, it means that oil revenues tend to be negligible in the economy.

The structure of the Algerian economy demonstrates its strong dependence on oil revenues. In the Mediterranean basin, Algeria is the leading energy power as a producer and exporter of oil and natural gas. Algerian natural gas accounts for around 50% of the total reserves of all the Mediterranean countries, 48% of total production and more than 95% of total exports. Algeria is one of the European Union's leading suppliers of natural gas.

Projects, plans, forecasts, budget financing, decisions, imports and even food and medicines are financed with hydrocarbon resources. Any event that shakes up international demand or causes a lasting drop in oil prices would result in a sharp fall in export earnings, with adverse consequences for the Algerian economy.

Figure 2.10 shows that Algeria's oil dependency index follows the trend in oil prices. Indeed, following the oil boom in 1973, dependence began to be pronounced. The oil dependency index rose from 35% in 1970 to 61% in 1974, pushing the Algerian economy into the "abyss" of hydrocarbon rents. The stability of oil prices in constant terms from 1974 to 1978 was followed by stagnation in the index level. After the second oil boom in 1979, the index rose to 64.38% in 1980. That said, almost two-thirds of the national economy depends on oil revenues. From 1980 to 1985, the oil dependency index followed the slight and gradual fall in oil prices. From 1986 to 1988, the index averaged 44.8%. This fall in the dependency index is not the result of the performance of the national economy, nor of a revival of non-hydrocarbon sectors, but is the consequence of the oil crisis of 1986, which followed the fall in oil prices.

In fact, during this period, oil tax revenues and hydrocarbon GDP fell by more than 50%. At the same time, the share of hydrocarbon exports in total exports did not really change. The adoption of a new law relating to the hydrocarbons sector in 1986 (Law 86–14) and the acceleration in the rate of extraction of hydrocarbons brought the oil dependency index down to a level of 63% in 1991. From that year onwards, the index fluctuated slightly until it virtually stabilised at around 65% during the 2000s.

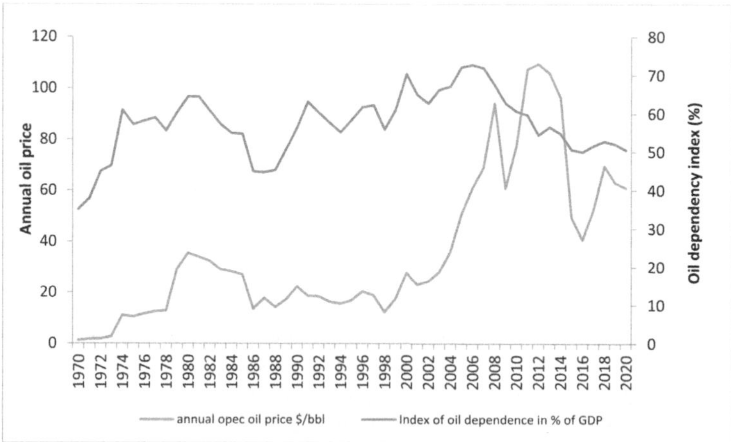

Figure 2.10 Trends in the oil dependency index and oil prices (1970–2020). Graph created by the author, compiled using data from ONS, Bank of Algeria, STATISTA, and the World Bank.

The upward trend of the 2000s accelerated, following the rise in oil prices until 2008, during the financial crisis when the price of a barrel rose from $53 in early 2007 to $145 in July 2008. The oil dependency index followed this upward trend, peaking in the years 2000 and 2008 at around 70%. After the oil shock of 2007–2008, when oil prices reached record levels, they fell once again to 36 dollars in December 2008, before rising again to reach 90 dollars at the beginning of 2011. With the counter-shock of 2014–2016, the price of a barrel of oil fell sharply to $63 at the end of June 2015, compared with $110 at the end of June 2014, a drop of 40%. The oil dependency index is also following this downward trend in oil prices.

All in all, the Algerian economy remains dependent on oil and gas revenues. It accounts for up to 98% of exports, 70% of budget revenue and 50% of GDP.

The issue of economic diversification is high on the agenda of governments in rentier economies. The aim is to reduce excessive dependence on a particular product, in this case, hydrocarbons. Pioneering work (Michaelly, 1958; Prebisch, 1950; Singer, 1950) has highlighted the role of diversification in protecting economies from excessive aggregate price shocks. Other works have also shown its role in controlling the vagaries of the economic cycle, particularly the fall in commodity prices for developing countries (Massel, 1970).

The Algerian economy remains massively dependent on the hydrocarbons sector, despite the political rhetoric about diversifying the national economy that has been developing since the late 1970s. After 50 years of trying, the country has not been able to undertake a structural transformation of its economy capable of extricating it from this dependence. The process of revitalising non-hydrocarbon growth is still at the planning stage.

2.3 The current state of economic diversification in Algeria

2.3.1 Export concentration index and number of products exported

The export concentration index measures the degree of sectoral concentration of a country's exports. It tells us whether a large proportion of a country's exports comes from a limited number of products or whether, on the contrary, they are spread more evenly across a larger number of products. Performance scores are distributed from 0 to 100. The lowest score indicates the best situation. The index has been standardised to obtain values between 0 and 1.

Figure 2.11 shows that the export concentration index (Herfindahl-Hirschman) indicates a very high level of export concentration, meaning that a large proportion of Algeria's exports come from a limited number of products. This index has been trending upwards since the early 2000s, peaking at 0.60 in 2006 and 2007, as the share of hydrocarbon exports in total exports peaked following the rise in hydrocarbon prices.

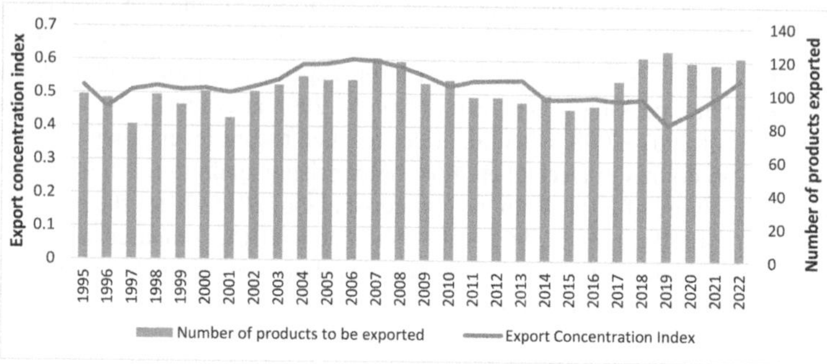

Figure 2.11 Comparative evolution of the export concentration index and the number of products exported in Algeria (1995–2022). Diagram created by the author, based on the author's own calculations using data from UNCTAD.

The Algerian economy is therefore highly specialised. The export concentration index is higher than all the averages for developing regions, including Africa (UNCTAD). It is comparable to that of other oil-exporting countries. The number of products exported remains very low, varying between 81 and 126. The country has not managed to open up new export lines, which are still largely dominated by hydrocarbons and derivatives, confirming the high concentration of exports.

The manufacturing sector plays an important role in economic theory. For classical economists, productivity in the manufacturing sector grew faster than in other economic activities. Keynesian theory placed the manufacturing sector at the heart of its theory. Investment in manufacturing is one of the surest ways for rentier economies to diversify. The weight of manufactured goods in a country's exports is thus one of the indicators of economic diversification. If this indicator is below 10%, it means that exports are essentially made up of raw products.

Figure 2.12 shows that Algeria is lagging far behind in exports of manufactured goods, and its share of total exports is very low. It represents an average of 2.3%, with a maximum of no more than 6% recorded in 1996. This shows Algeria's poor performance in exports of manufactured goods, while Morocco and Tunisia, which are very close geographically, have the same trading partners and are less endowed and much more diversified. Indeed, since the mid-1990s, the share of manufactured goods in total exports has exceeded 60% in Morocco and 80% in Tunisia, while manufactured exports have failed to take off in Algeria (Elsenhans, 2023).

The export capacity of Algeria's manufacturing industries, therefore, remains negligible. Algeria's premature de-industrialisation has further complicated the reconciliation of diversification and integration into the global economy. The manufacturing sector, a lever for diversification par excellence, is constrained by the international environment, which in fact heavily regulates and

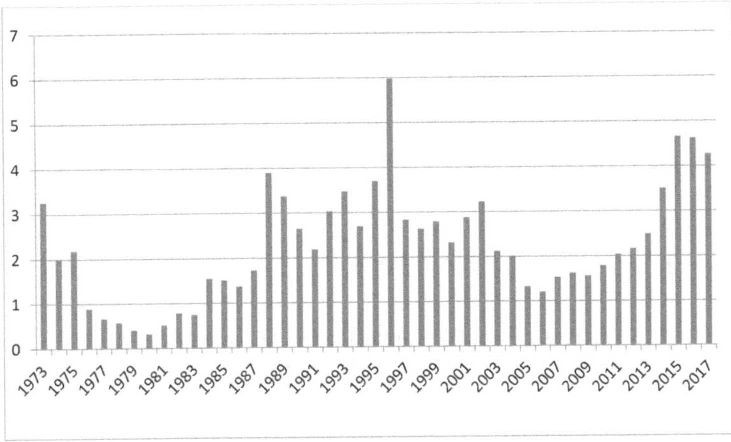

Figure 2.12 Exports of manufactured goods as a proportion of all goods exported in Algeria (1973–2018). Diagram created by the author, based on the author's own calculations using BP data.

prohibits the use of industrial policy instruments implemented in the past by developed and emerging countries (UNCTAD, 2017, p. 55). Foreign trade in manufactured products accounts for almost 100% of inter-industry trade, with an index that varies between 0.94 and 0.99. This means that the manufacturing industry is almost exclusively an importer (UNCTAD, 2017, p. 47). Exports of high-technology goods, which reflect the country's ability to design, produce and export increasingly sophisticated goods, thus requiring higher and higher labour qualifications (human capital), the use of ICTs and compliance with standards are non-existent in Algeria (World Bank).

2.3.2 Algeria's export diversification index

The diversification index measures the absolute deviation of a country's export product structure from the world structure. Its value lies between 0 and 1. The closer the index is to 1, the greater the deviation from the world structure. Figure 2.13 shows that in the case of Algeria, the diversification index remains virtually stable, with small variations and values varying between 0.72 and 0.87.

Given the predominant weight of hydrocarbons in GDP and exports, the country is on the fringes of global value chains, currently considered to be an essential vector of trade. This shows that the structure of trade is very specific compared with the world average. This has a considerable impact on Algeria's ranking in the economic complexity index, which measures the degree of economic sophistication of its exports. Algeria ranks 108th out of 127 countries, while Morocco ranks 90th and Tunisia 44th.

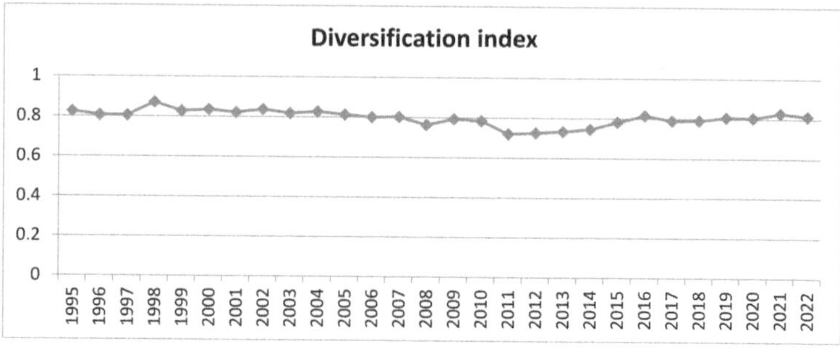

Figure 2.13 Algeria's export diversification index for the period 1995–2022. Graph produced by the author, using data provided by the World Bank.

2.3.3 Import concentration index and number of products imported into Algeria

The import concentration index measures, for each country, the degree of concentration of imported products. It tells us whether a country's imports depend on a limited number of products or whether, on the contrary, they are spread more evenly across a large number of products.

Figure 2.14 shows the comparative evolution of the import concentration index and the number of products imported into Algeria over the period

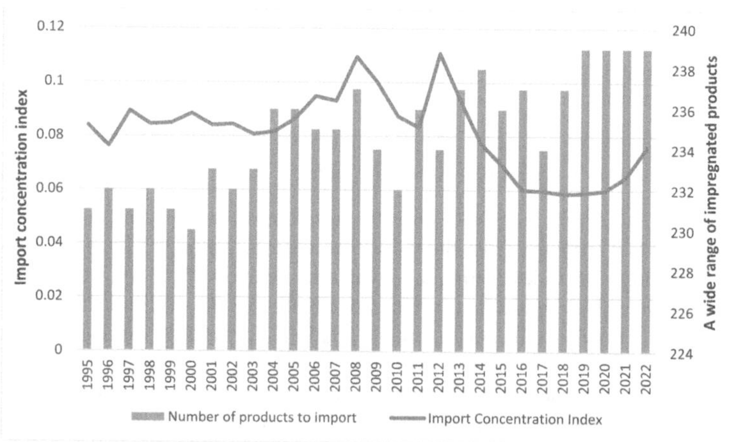

Figure 2.14 Comparative evolution of the import concentration index and the number of products imported into Algeria (1995–2022). Diagram created by the author, based on the author's calculations using UNCTAD data.

1995–2018. From this figure, we can see that the import concentration index in Algeria is very low, peaking in 2012 at 0.11, then falling to 0.05 in 2018. This means that Algeria's imports are spread across a large number of products. Indeed, the number of products imported into Algeria confirms this, with very high values ranging from 230 to 239. Products intended for industry (semi-finished and finished products) account for the largest share of imports. The manufacturing industry is the largest importer in the Algerian economy, accounting for more than 80% of total imports, and more than 97% of all industrial imports, including hydrocarbons.

2.4 Conclusion

In a context characterised by the gradual reduction in the country's hydrocarbon export revenues and a national economy characterised by the small size of its non-hydrocarbon productive sector. Indeed, non-hydrocarbon exports remain low, marginal and represent a very small volume. More than 80% of exports are concentrated on hydrocarbons, and dependence on imports is growing.

Algeria's degree of export concentration is among the highest in the world. The number of products exported remains very low, and the country is unable to open up new export lines, which are still largely dominated by hydrocarbons and derivatives, confirming the high concentration of exports. Algeria is also lagging far behind in exports of manufactured goods, and its share of total exports is very low. As for the import concentration index, it is very low in Algeria, which means that imports are spread across a large number of products. In fact, the number of products imported confirms this, with very high values.

Products intended for industry (semi-finished and finished products) account for the largest share of imports. This asymmetry between the uniqueness of exports and the diversity of imports makes the Algerian economy highly vulnerable to the disruptions that cyclically affect the hydrocarbon market and the dollar. We thus confirm that the Algerian economy is characterised by poor diversification of the productive base and exports, and its economic performance is excessively dependent on the hydrocarbon sector. If the country is unable to diversify its economy, it is because it comes up against a number of very complex constraints, such as a weak structural transformation of the economy, an unfavourable institutional framework and business climate, and a derisory size of the private sector.

Notes

1 Statistics from the Office for National Statistics (ONS) 2023. The figures are available on the ONS website: https://www.ons.dz/
2 Algérie Presse Service (APS): Document published by APS and available on the Algérie Presse Service (APS) website: https://www.aps.dz/economie/74476-gaz-de-schiste
3 Over 90% probability of recovery

References

Acosta, A. (2013). Extractivism and neoextractivism: Two sides of the same curse. In M. Lang & D. Mokrani (Eds.), Beyond Development: Alternative Visions from Latin America (pp. 61–86). Amsterdam: Transnational Institute.

Acosta, A. (2015). El Buen Vivir: Sumak Kawsay, una oportunidad para imaginar otros mundos. Barcelona: Icaria.

Auty, R. (1993). Sustaining development in mineral economies: The resource curse thesis.

Beblawi, H. (1987). The Rentier State in the Arab World. *Arab Studies Quarterly*, *9*(4), 383–398. http://www.jstor.org/stable/41857943

Beblawi, H. (1990). The Rentier State in the Arab World. In G. Luciani (Ed.), The Arab State (pp. 85–98). London: Routledge.

Beblawi, H., & Luciani, G. (Eds.). (1987). The Rentier State. London: Croom Helm.

Beblawi, H., & Luciani, G. (2015). The Rentier State. Routledge Library Editions: Politics of the Middle-East.

Brand, U., & Wissen, M. (2013). Crisis and continuity of capitalist society-nature relationships: The imperial mode of living and the limits to environmental governance. Review of International Political Economy, 20(4), 687–711.

Dahmani, A. (2015). Les ressources naturelles dans les pays en développement: moteur de croissance ou élément de vulnérabilité économique. De l'industrialisation àl'économie de rente: l'expérience algérienne des années 1970.

Elsenhans, H. (1982). Abhängiger Kapitalismus oder bürokratische Entwicklungsgesellschaft. Frankfurt: Suhrkamp.

Elsenhans, H. (2023). Capitalism and Rent, a Destructive Relationship: Why the Maghreb Does not Join the Newly Industrializing Countries. Tunis: Arabesques Editions.

Farzin, Y. (1992, July). The Time Path Rent in Theory of Exhaustible Resources. The Economic Journal, 102(413), 813–830.

Gelb, A. H. (1988). Windfall Gains: Blessing or Curse? New York: Oxford University Press.

Gudynas, E. (2009). Ten theses on new extractivism. Extractivism Working Paper, CLAES.

Herb, M. (2005). No Representation without Taxation? Rents, Development, and Democracy. *Comparative Politics*, *37*(3), 297–316. https://doi.org/10.2307/20072891

Mahdavy, H. (1970). The patterns and problems of economic development in rentier states: The case of Iran. In M. A. Cook (Ed.), Studies in the Economic History of the Middle East (pp. 428–467). London: Oxford University Press.

Massel, F. (1970). Export instability and economic structure. American Economic Review, 60(4), 618–630.

Michaelly, M. (1958). Concentration of export and imports: An international comparison. Economic Journal, 68, 722–736.

Mouhoubi, A. (2012). La gestion de la rente des ressources naturelles épuisables dans la perspective du développement économique [Doctoral Dissertation, Université de Béjaïa].

Nankany, G. T. (1979). Development Problems of Mineral Exporting Countries. World Bank. Staff Working Paper, 354.

Ouaissa, R. (2010). La Classe-État algérienne 1962–2000. Une histoire du pouvoir algérien entre sous-développement, rente pétrolière et terrorisme. Paris: Publisud éditions.

Power, M., Newell, P., Baker, L., et al. (2016). The political economy of energy transitions in Mozambique and South Africa: The role of the Rising Powers. Energy Research & Social Science, 17, 10–19.

Prebisch, R. (1950). Economic Development of Latin America and its Principal Problems. New York: United Nations, Lake Success.

Ross, M. (2001). Does oil hinder democracy? World Politics, 53(3), 325–361.

Singer, H. W. (1950). U.S. Foreign Investment in Underdeveloped Areas: The distribution of gains between investing and borrowing countries. American Economic Review, 40(2), 473–485.

Smith, A. (1968, June). Economics of production from natural resources. The American Economic Review, 58(3), 409–431.

Svampa, M. (2019). Neo-extractivism in Latin America: Socio-environmental Conflicts, the Territorial Turn, and New Political Narratives. Cambridge: Cambridge University Press.

United Nations Conference on Trade and Development (UNCTAD). (2017). *World investment report 2017: Investment and the digital economy.* United Nations. https://unctad.org/system/files/official-document/wir2017_en.pdf

3 The administered economy

1962–1988

3.1 Introduction

In the previous chapter, we noted the structural nature of the domination of hydrocarbons in the system of accumulation in Algeria. Our aim in this chapter and the next is to shed light on the origins of this situation. To do so, we will go back to the political and economic choices made by the Algerian state following independence in 1962 and their main results.

A French colony for a century and thirty-two years, Algeria inherited a colonial-style economic structure after independence, where the "development of the territory" was based on the economic interests of the metropolis and the European minority living on Algerian soil. These characteristics can be summed up as follows: under-industrialisation, dualism in the agricultural sector and financial and commercial dependence on metropolitan France.

Like most formerly colonised countries, Algeria decided to break away from its "colonial economy," which was seen as the main source of its underdevelopment. This break was to be materialised in two ways. Politically, the new state opted for a single-party system and a centrally planned economy. Secondly, the Algerian authorities decided to focus the national development strategy on industry, largely neglecting the agricultural sector, which was already at a very advanced stage of modernisation.

This model took the form of the state control of economic activities, the suppression of the autonomy of economic agents, and the extreme centralisation of resource allocation. According to the leaders of the 1960s, centralised planning and massive public investment, particularly in industry, were the only way for Algeria to emerge from underdevelopment. In fact, from the mid-1960s to the late 1970s, Algeria underwent a radical policy of nationalisation, colossal public investment and radical questioning of all economic, monetary and trade union powers. In other words, it was a question of mobilising all resources to develop the country through industry without the intervention of the market, or rather against the laws of the market.

The results of voluntarism as an economic practice were far from the proclaimed objectives. The market, which the state had fought for years, took its

DOI: 10.4324/9781003665571-4

revenge by doubling its prices, making the planner's administrative directives irrelevant. Instead of an industrial and productive economy, Algeria found itself, towards the end of the 1970s, with a rentier economy, distributing wealth that it did not create—much of it circulating in the informal market.

This chapter is divided into three sections: the first aims to identify the main manifestations of voluntarism that inspired the economic practices of the Algerian state during the 1960s and 1970s. This will involve a presentation of the various actions taken by the Algerian state to put into effect the development strategy it set itself the task of implementing, whatever the cost. The second section looks at the corrective measures taken under the Algerian Development Strategy of the early 1980s and their results. The third section is devoted to the first experiment in market transition, designed and implemented by the reformist government led by Mouloud Hamrouche in the early 1990s.

3.2 The proactive economy of the 1960s and 1970s

The economic voluntarism that underpinned the State's practices during the 1960s and 1970s was expressed through the implementation of what is commonly referred to as the Algerian Development Strategy (Stratégie Algérienne du Développement, SAD). These different manifestations could be seen in the content of the economic model adopted, but also and above all in the scale of the resources deployed by the State to achieve it.

In fact, a few years after independence, precisely after the coup d'Etat of 19 June 1965, the State's economic choices were refined and radicalised. Development became state-run, industrial and centrally planned. This marked the beginning of a long process of nationalisation of sources of wealth. In the space of a few years, State control spread to all sectors of activity, from industry and agriculture to domestic and foreign trade. Businesses, banks and insurance companies were all placed under ministerial supervision. It was a massive transfer of wealth from civil society to the State.

Encouraged by substantial oil revenues following the nationalisation of hydrocarbons, the State built its strategy on massive public investment across all sectors of activity. Also, in accordance with the principles of development through planning, it is the State itself which has been responsible for defining the variables for regulating the flow and reflux of wealth: prices, interest rates, exchange rates and wages are defined in advance by the planning body. In this way, the entire political and administrative environment governing the economic sphere has been completely transformed in order to bring the economic society under State control.

Moreover, monetary power was brought under the political authority of the Central Bank of Algeria in 1964. As a result, monetary policy was conceived not in terms of the instruments and objectives defined by economic theory, but in terms of the financing needs of the development plans drawn up centrally by the political authorities.

3.2.1 State-controlled economy, centralised planning and sectoral policies in favour of industry

In accordance with the chosen political and economic model, Algeria embarked on a policy of extreme State control of its economy in the early years of its independence. In economic terms, the industrial choices made by the planners largely determined the nature of the organisation governing the Algerian economic system. Industrialising industries have two characteristics: they are highly capital-intensive and not very profitable in the short or medium term. Consequently, only the State is capable of developing them. To achieve this, a vast movement to nationalise wealth was set in motion, and gigantic monopolies were created—the Sociétés Nationales—to control and manage all sectors of activity, from production to supply and distribution.

The State's objective was to dissolve all economic structures into a large administrative organisation so that the planner could intervene at every stage of the development process. Advance planning, downstream public investment and upstream control of all economic activities, all driven by the industrial sector. These were the broad outlines that defined the state process for implementing SAD.

A Centrally Planned Economy (CPE) is defined by directive planning of the economy, public ownership of companies and banks, collectivisation of agriculture, a development strategy based on accelerated industrialisation, the quest for commercial autarchy and a ban on direct foreign investment. The CPE is organised on a hierarchical basis, headed by a planning centre which sends directives to the various supervisory ministries, which in turn pass them on to State companies. The investments to be made and the budgets required for them were determined on the basis of a pre-established plan. It is the State, through its various administrative structures, that is replacing market-based regulation.

By definition, a so-called administered economy means the negation of economic agents in the sense suggested by political economy. Since they have no autonomy from political supervision, economic agents cannot organise themselves economically or politically to defend their interests; they are passive players. In countries with an administered economy run by a single party—often with a populist ideology—the unity of the people is proclaimed around the central objectives of the development plan, and no one is expected to defend their interests according to their social class, profession, etc. In this way, all powers (economic, political, social, etc.) are exercised by the same people. In this way, all powers (economic, trade union, monetary, etc.) are combated by the State in the name of imperative national construction. For example, companies could not dismiss workers, but neither could workers form autonomous trade unions to defend their socio-occupational rights. Economic and social activity developed entirely through and around the State, including the activities of the national private sector, whose interests were closely linked to the political authority.

This organisational scheme, defined above, was adopted in Algeria. The organisation and operation of the economic system put in place immediately after independence in 1962, and reinforced after the coup d'Etat in 1965, were not based on any independent economic institution. The Central Bank and the banking sector were in the hands of the State. Public enterprises and chambers of commerce and industry were organised and managed like any other government department. Their role was to carry out the decisions taken as part of the plan drawn up at the top of the State.

The institutional functioning of this model is based on a pyramid: the centre—the place where decisions are taken—is occupied by the State's political institutions (the Presidency, the Revolutionary Council and a number of powerful ministries such as Finance and Industry). The second level is represented by the central administration, the supervisory ministries and the Central Bank. It acts as a transmission belt between the centre and the economic agents, without any real decision-making power. Finally comes the implementation centre. It is responsible for scrupulously implementing the wishes of the hierarchy. At this level are public companies and the various monetary and financial institutions that are legally owned by the State. They are therefore at the State's disposal to implement its development projects. In this respect, the 1976 National Charter clearly stipulated that: "*the socialist economy implies first and foremost the intervention, through national planning, of political power, which must guide economic, social and cultural action*" (National Charter, 1976, p. 140). This imperative guidance of economic action conferred on political power by the various texts that have marked the political and economic life of the country (constitution, various national charters, etc.) has resulted in the abolition of all autonomy for economic agents.

By way of illustration, public companies in Algeria were owned by the State, which was not only present through its capital, but also intervened in all the company's functions through the supervisory ministries. Public companies had neither legal personality nor financial autonomy, as was the case for companies in mixed economies. With no legal means of taking decisions that fell within the classic attributes of an economic unit, the public enterprise in Algeria was, as Addi points out (Addi, 1990, p. 213), "*a political-administrative unit charged with economic functions.*" This transfer of economic power from public companies to the supervisory ministries was officially enshrined in the charter for the socialist organisation of companies, commonly known as Gestion Socialiste des Entreprises (GSE) of December 1971.

Similarly, almost all the institutions responsible for financing the economy belonged to the public sector. Commercial banks received their resources directly from the State, which was legally their owner and manager. Like the rest of the public enterprises and state-owned firms, they obeyed the administrative orders of the central authority. In the Algerian development experience, the power to direct investment flows and/or monetary flows through interest, discount and rediscount rates did not lie with the banks. This is why it is inappropriate to consider monetary and financial institutions in a system of imperative planning as economic agents in their own right. Algerian public banks were politico-administrative entities (like the rest of the public enterprises) responsible for monetary and financial functions. The role of these institutions in Algeria's economic organisation was to ensure the system's major balances. They were the main channel through which the State's distributive function operated. In other words, the banks were required to finance investments under the plan and to provide permanent working capital for public enterprises, which were often in deficit.

In addition, trade union representation was prohibited in the name of the community of interest between the State and the workers. In the socialist public enterprise, "*the interests of the State and those of the producers are inseparable,*"[1] the National Charter emphasises. Consequently, no expression was conceivable outside the official trade union (UGTA), whose status was closer to that of a mass organisation than that of a trade union. By legalising the transfer of economic power from the company to the State, the Socialist Management of Enterprises (GSE) gave workers the impression that they were participating in the effective management of their companies. In reality, neither management nor workers could take the slightest decision, because the company as a whole had no decision-making power. But this had the advantage of avoiding the need for the State to arbitrate in conflicts between labour and capital, and this was no small advantage for a State that wanted to unify the social body as part of the "nation-building" undertaking.

Through the few indications outlined above, we wish to give an idea of the decision-making hierarchy which presides over the Algerian economic organisation under the centralised planning system. The latter was entirely in the hands of the state: having been divested of all power, economic agents were seen as passive players responding to the administration's injunctions. The allocation and assignment of resources were the exclusive responsibility of the political authority, embodied by the single-party regime: this is why we speak of an administered economy when we talk about the economic history of Algeria during this period.

The State's economic voluntarism, the main manifestations of which were discussed above, has also been expressed in the scale of public investment, its sectoral allocation and the sources chosen by the State to finance it.

In terms of investment, the State invested DA 300 billion (half of it in foreign currency) between 1967 and 1978. The ratio of public investment to GDP rose from 26% between 1967 and 1969 to over 50% in 1978/1979. The share of total investment allocated to the industrial sector (including hydrocarbons) is dominant. Indeed, after having been around 53.4%

(i.e., 4.9 million DA) during the three-year plan (1967–1969), the share of industrial investment rose to 61.1% (71.1 million DA) between 1974 and 1977, i.e., more than half of the investments made during the decade. Compared with industry, agriculture and services were left at the bottom of the planner's priorities. In percentage terms, agriculture, which after independence was the leading foreign exchange earner, received only 20.7% of the investment provided for in the three-year plan. Worse still, this tiny share was reduced to just 7.3%, or 8.9 million DA, during the second four-year plan. This explains the gradual decline of Algeria's agricultural sector, which, a few decades later, caused the country to become one of the biggest importers of food products worldwide.[2]

But let's make no mistake: more than 50% of these colossal investments in the industrial sector have been taken up by hydrocarbons. This figure was 60% in 1979. On this subject, A. Dahmani (1999, pp. 32–3) speaks of the "perversion" of the industrialisation model: "*rather than failure, it would be more accurate to speak of the 'perversion' of the industrialisation model and the development of a rentier and dependent economy,*" before adding that the only change experienced by the Algerian economy after the implementation of three development plans was the replacement of agriculture by hydrocarbons: "*the only change was that agriculture was replaced by oil, the sub-soil replaced the soil. However, in the development project, industrialisation is the strategic element.*"

As for the financing of these colossal investments, it is clear that the State monopolises oil revenues. An analysis of the share of oil taxes in the State budget is significant in this respect. It shows the steady increase—in contrast to ordinary taxation—in the proportion of the State budget accounted for by oil taxation. It rose from 12% between 1963 and 1966 to over 57% in 1978 and 1979.

In addition, the role of oil revenues in financing investment in Algeria can be illustrated, not just by their contribution to the State budget, but by direct comparison with the volume of public investment. In terms of percentage, from 1971 onwards, the share of investment allocated to the hydrocarbons sector has risen steadily. It should be noted that the rate rose from 42.95% in 1970 to 71.35% in 1979, i.e. almost 15 years after the launch of the SAD. Second, the volume of investment increased each time foreign exchange earnings improved, as was the case during the two oil crises. For example, the sudden rise in the volume of investment from DA 6,296 million in 1973 to DA 17,965 million in 1974 was only possible because hydrocarbon exports had risen from DA 12,417.5 million to DA 16,964.4 million. This begs the question as to why the Algerian State regularly increased the volume of investment each time its foreign exchange earnings improved, when the economy was supposed to be managed according to the principles of planning; in other words, the volume of investment had already been defined before the increase in international hydrocarbon prices! The answer to this question is twofold.

First, planning in Algeria is an empty word. In practice, the leaders rarely respected the recommendations of the planning body, the National Planning Secretariat. "*It was a smokescreen, a Kafkaesque situation,*" *as* Dahmani (1999, p. 39) puts it. Dahmani relies on the testimony of G. Hidouci, who states that "*It was a well-run, well-managed administration (Le Plan) which pretended to play the role assigned to it... our game consisted in tinkering with the figures and official recommendations, always in three versions: the first, cautious, for the President; the second, more or less sincere, for internal use; the third, downright manipulated, for working relations with the ministries. We always had to prove to them that there was no money.*"

Proof of the lack of interest shown by Algerian leaders in planning can be seen in the constant overspending and over-investment in the various plans. The second reason for this systematic increase in investment, in parallel with the rise in hydrocarbon prices, lies in the scale of the additional costs and the Remainder To Be Achieved (RAA). In fact, none of the development plans that have been implemented have achieved their objectives. This is why the State regularly increased the volume of its investments each time the financial situation improved, in order to make up for the shortcomings of the previous plans, all of which were covered by oil revenues. Oil revenues were the first and main source of funding for SAD.

The preponderance of oil revenues in the financing of SAD can be justified by the weakness of the capital base in the various sectors of the Algerian economy following independence. After colonisation, Algeria was in such a state of underdevelopment that no sector of activity was sufficiently developed to generate the resources needed to launch a process of industrialisation. But this gradual "petrolisation" of the State budget after 15 years of launching the SAD requires an explanation other than the weakness of local capital. Part of the explanation lies in the government's tendency to favour investment in the hydrocarbons sector to the detriment of industries that are properly industrialising. Indeed, the oil sector has always been the main focus of State industrial investment, to the point where some authors speak of a perversion of the industrial model.

In fact, statistical data on the distribution of public investment by branch of activity shows that there was a flagrant imbalance in favour of hydrocarbons; the share of investment in hydrocarbons in planned investment was around 45% during the first four-year plan, 47% during the second four-year plan and 55% during the two years 1978 and 1979 without a plan, which were described as the years of pause. In this respect, the following question arises: why did the State invest so much in a sector which was supposed to be only a "transitory" supplier of investments prior to the beginning of the dynamics of accumulation by industry?

In reality, the state was caught in a trap. To finance its development strategy, it had to invest in the hydrocarbons sector, but faced with the lack of return on investment reflected in the deficit of state-owned companies, it was obliged to invest even more in hydrocarbons to avoid "bankruptcy." This assertion can be justified by the observation of two phenomena: the first relates to the ever-increasing revision of investments in favour of hydrocarbons compared with those that were planned; the second concerns the privileged activities within the hydrocarbons sector itself. It should be noted that the State gives priority to export-oriented activities to the detriment of "industrialising" functions.

In fact, a closer analysis of the investments made in the hydrocarbon sector shows that the State was looking for "new money" rather than investment in the industrialising branches of the hydrocarbon industry. The priority activities financed within the hydrocarbons sector were those known as exporting, because they were the ones that immediately provided the capital in foreign currency.

The contradictions in which the State found itself when it came to implementing the SAD were clear to see. To make up the deficit in the productive sector, it was necessary to invest more in hydrocarbons. In so doing, the rentier sphere invaded the productive sphere and prevented it from triggering any dynamic of accumulation. Algeria's subsequent economic history amply confirms this: the hydrocarbons sector has gradually become so independent of the rest of the economy that it is no exaggeration to speak of "an economy within an economy."

3.2.2 Results and contradictions of the administered economy

The assessments of the SAD are many and varied, and their conclusions are unanimous: state investment was significant and widespread across all sectors of activity, but the economic and social results were far from the stated objectives. No sector was spared, from industry to agriculture, not to mention the socio-economic conditions of the population. Worse still, the State's pro-active economic policy has led the national economy to become doubly dependent—on energy rents and foreign debt—coupled with a structural inflationary situation due to the "irrational" expansion of the money supply. In this way, all the contradictions of the administered economy were brought out into the open.

What is striking about the Algerian economy is the inability of public companies to reproduce their own capital. This is despite the fact that they were initially endowed with equity capital by the state, and that the state assumed all costs relating to investments. Worse still, despite the repeated reduction in their debts, Algerian public companies, with a few exceptions, were running large and permanent deficits. Compared with the volume of investments made by the State, this deficit cannot be explained solely by the conceptual tools of economic theory. Consequently, its analysis requires us to take into account the socio-political environment in which these companies were operating. In other words, Algerian companies were immersed in an institutional environment which, from a strictly economic point of view, was hostile to the minimum conditions for profitability. We will come back to this in the following sections.

State investment between 1967 and 1978 amounted to AD 300 billion (1978 value), half of which was in foreign currency. Over the same period, this colossal sum only gave rise to additional production of 46.5 billion dinars, or only 15.5% of total investment. With the exception of the hydrocarbons sector, the deficit in the industrial sector rose from 408 million DA in 1973 to 1880 million DA in 1978 (Addi, 1990).

At 31 December 1978, the accumulated debt of state-owned companies (all sectors combined) totalled DA 179 billion. This was double the value of GDP, which was DA 86.8 billion in the same year. Most of this debt was irrecoverable. According to calculations provided by A. Brahimi, Algerian public companies were only able to repay 4.8% of the initial debt of D198 billion up to 1978. Ironically, the former Algerian Prime Minister in the 1980s, A. Brahimi, declared that "*it would take national companies almost two centuries to pay off this debt, assuming that they had stopped borrowing in 1978, which is obviously unimaginable*" (Brahimi, 1991). Indeed, public enterprises have not stopped borrowing, but their deficits have been intensifying.

Furthermore, the average annual growth rate of agricultural production was only 2.4% between 1967 and 1978. This was well below the rate of population growth, estimated at 3.2%. As a proportion of GDP, agriculture accounted for just 8% in 1978, down from 13% in 1967. This imbalance between agricultural production and population growth led to increased food dependency: between 1975 and 1979, Algeria imported the equivalent of 61% of its cereal consumption, the largest item in its food imports. Cereal imports represented an annual average of 20% of total imports. The food trade coverage rate, which was 50% at the end of the 1960s, fell sharply to just 0.6% in the mid-1980s.

Analysis of the structure of Algeria's foreign trade is one of the most telling indicators of the extent to which the Algerian economy is dependent on both its oil resources and imports. A study of the structure of Algerian imports and exports during this period shows the weakness of local supply, the importance of national demand for imported products and the importance of oil revenues in covering the trade deficit (Chapter 1).

Another important element to highlight is the question of monetary management. An analysis of the Algerian State's monetary concepts and policies reveals, more than any other study, the expression of the voluntarism which motivated state development practices, and the contradictions to which it gave rise. So much so that, just a few years after the introduction of the SAD, the national production system found itself faced with a structural accounting deficit, making its dependence on oil revenues inevitable right up to the present day. The reason for this is that the development process was conducted primarily in terms of physical quantities, relegating monetary and financial phenomena to second place.

To take just one example, statistics show that money creation from loans to the economy fell from 72% between 1970 and 1973 to 56% between 1978 and 1979. By contrast, claims on the State more than tripled, rising from 10% between 1970 and 1973 to 37% between 1978 and 1979. This trend is somewhat paradoxical given that the country has already implemented three development plans. As for foreign assets, they represented a small proportion of these counterparts, as the figures show (18% from 1970 to 1973 and 9% in 1979), which means that assets were no longer a source of monetary creation but of destruction due to the fall in foreign exchange reserves. This expansion of the money supply without any productive counterpart in goods and services resulted in a constantly rising inflation rate. It rose by a staggering 105.7% between 1974 and 1978, compared with 23% in eight years (1967/74).[3]

This predominance of quantitative planning and the resulting subordination of money produced a dichotomy between the circulation of money and the movement of real assets. The separate evolution of monetary expansion and its counterpart in goods and services has plunged the entire economy into an inflationary process, which has eroded the purchasing power of the underprivileged social strata while reinforcing the transfer of wealth to the private sector. These two results are in total contradiction with the objectives that the State had set itself through the establishment of the SAD, namely, social justice and industrialisation by the public sector.

On the basis of the figures presented in the previous section, we note that after some 15 years of active implementation of its development strategy, Algeria has not succeeded in establishing a productive economic system, i.e., organising its economy by building a national market capable of creating wealth and distributing it throughout society in accordance with the laws of political economy. The country's economic sectors did not produce added value, and rents permeated all economic and social relations. At the end of the 1970s, the Algerian economy functioned essentially thanks to the income generated by the export of hydrocarbons. It distributed wealth that it did not create.

The process of creating a rentier, distributive economy in Algeria is a direct consequence of the State's economic practices. This result, although unexpected, is that of an ideological conception generating economic practices, and having hampered the mechanisms of wealth creation and the dynamics of accumulation. Thus, the proliferation of rents and rentier positions produced by the nature of the articulation imposed by the political regime between relations of power (political, social and symbolic) and economic relations, has turned the Algerian economic space into a determined and non-determining space.

To put it another way, the deliberate embedding of the economic sphere in the political sphere, reflected in the transfer of economic power from civil society and its domiciliation in the political sphere, has meant that the economic sphere has not operated according to its own rationality. The Algerian economic sphere has been subject to the political logic of the holder of resources and the decision to allocate them, in this case, the State. This was the logic of the administered economy adopted by the Algerian state immediately after independence.

The crisis of the Algerian economic system is that of a type of organisation in which rents are the dominant social relationship. While the social strata dominated by the rentier system have developed complex strategies to capture the maximum amount of state income, the anonymous market forces unleashed by the permanent injection of income, in accordance with the mechanisms of the administered economy and the logic of the rentier state, have profoundly transformed society, sharpening its contradictions and generating a deep crisis in the social bond.

By trying "at all costs" to build an economy sheltered from the market, the State has provoked a vicious cycle of public enterprise deficits, monetary expansion/inflation, market segmentation and the emergence of a parallel economy, all topped off by the "democratisation" of corruption as a means of enriching oneself by holding the public and private sectors to ransom indiscriminately.

3.3 From initial restructuring to open crisis (1980–1988)

The official slogan of Ch. Ben Jedid's first "mandate" perfectly summed up the spirit of the economic reforms of the early 1980s: "*Change within continuity.*" Change was necessary because the previous development strategy had just lost its main architect, H. Boumediene. The promised economic take-off was slow in coming, and the socio-economic situation of the population continued to deteriorate. But continuity was also essential because the political regime had no intention of departing from its political and ideological conceptions of the organisation and functions of the economic system. The result was that continuity took precedence over change. First of all, it should be remembered that the day after the death of H. Boumediene, the new management team led by Ch. Ben Jedid carried out an economic and social review of the experience of the 1970s. The conclusions of this review, the first of its kind in independent Algeria, were critical for the "industrialists," whose political influence was unparalleled from the coup d'état of June 1965 until Boumediene's death in December 1978.

By way of a solution, the new management team proposed a series of changes officially described as "reforms." The results of this "new" economic direction were, in the unanimous opinion of observers, below the stated objectives.

Along the way, Algeria was hit hard by the oil shock in 1986: the simultaneous fall in oil prices and the value of the US dollar immediately caused foreign currency earnings to fall by almost half. Economic reforms were once again needed. The State had to find urgent and, why not, radical solutions to its economic problems, the persistence of which directly threatened the political stability of the regime. It was against this backdrop that, in 1987, a think-tank was set up under the leadership of Mouloud Hamrouche, then Secretary General of the Government and then of the Presidency. The task force's mission was to find appropriate solutions to the dysfunctions of the Algerian economy.

3.3.1 The redevelopments of the early 1980s/1986

The "adjustments" made to the Algerian Development Strategy can be summed up in three main areas: rebalancing the weight of economic sectors, the internal reorganisation of public companies, and the redefinition of the role of the national private sector. According to the official discourse, there were two main objectives. The first was to consolidate the structures of the national economy by means of an imperative but decentralised planning system. Secondly, it was intended to eliminate the obstacles to the efficient management of public companies by restructuring them organically and financially. All of this was to result in the spread of development throughout the country and across all sectors of activity.

As far as rebalancing the economic system is concerned, it should be remembered that as part of the assessment of the national economy carried out at the end of the 1970s, some Algerian leaders rightly noted an imbalance in the allocation of resources between the various sectors of activity. By way of solution, the designers of the five-year plan (1980–1984) attempted a new development policy based on the concept of "rebalancing." The aim was to redirect economic policy in favour of sectors deemed to be "lagging behind" the industrial sector, such as agriculture, water and other economic and social infrastructures.

The second and undoubtedly most important aspect of the "reorganisation" carried out in the early 1980s was the organic and financial restructuring of public companies. This operation was undertaken between February 1981 and 1 January 1984. It resulted in the break-up of the 70 major national companies across all sectors into more than 400 national and regional companies. In parallel with this operation, a financial restructuring was undertaken at the beginning of 1983. This action was justified, on the one hand, by the need to resolve the problem of the chronic accounting deficit of state-owned companies and, on the other hand, by the need to distribute assets and liabilities between the old companies and the new companies created by the organic restructuring underway. The financial restructuring of public companies was based, depending on the case, on three axes: the endowment of the newly created company with equity capital, the transformation of the debt of existing companies into a definitive endowment when the debt is long-term and into consolidation for short-term debts; finally, the gradual settlement of inter-company debts.

In reality, this financial restructuring of public companies was nothing more than an operation to dry up the debts accumulated as a result of successive deficits. It often consisted of simply writing off the accumulated debts by transferring them to the State, and sometimes rescheduling the outstanding debt with the intervention of the Treasury, which amounts to practically the same thing.

3.3.2 Economic assessment of the "corrective" SAD reforms

At the risk of being repetitive, let's recall the most important actions recommended to rebalance the sectoral distribution of investment. It was decided to favour agriculture and services, to avoid costly and uncontrollable technological choices and to satisfy as many of the population's social needs as possible. But the actual practices of the Algerian decision-makers were at odds with the stated objectives.

The sectoral reallocation of investment did not favour agriculture as expected. According to available statistics, the share of industrial investment in total investment has remained high, while that of agriculture has not changed sufficiently. In this respect, it should be pointed out that in absolute terms, agriculture and water supply received billions of Dinars, 47 in 1980–1984 compared with only 15.2 in 1974–77. However, in relative terms and for the same periods, the figures are literally reversed: 11.7% in 80–84 compared with 15.2% in 74–77. In fact, the weight of the old strategy remained significant despite the desire to reverse the trend: the importance of the industrial sector and the Remainders to Achieve from the old plans made any attempt to change course problematic. As an illustration, the project officially aimed at modernising agriculture has remained a dead letter.

As far as the second axis of reform is concerned, i.e., the financial and organic restructuring of state-owned enterprises and farms, the analyses provided on this subject are unanimous: the quest for "autonomous" economic growth in the hydrocarbon sector has not produced the expected results, and the deficit of state-owned enterprises and farms has continued to grow. Given that the principles of Socialist Enterprise Management prohibited cuts in the workforce or other social charges, the reduction in the volume of industrial investment was essentially achieved through lower purchases of equipment. The significant reduction in equipment imports, despite the fact that they were necessary for the operation of the industrial complexes that had already been set up, ultimately only contributed to reinforcing the under-exploitation of national production capacity, considered in the 1979 balance sheet to be a major source of industrial inefficiency!

In the end, continuity prevailed over change, and the state system continued to operate according to the same practices, with worsening results. Between

1984 and 1987, the non-hydrocarbon operating deficit of public enterprises was estimated at DA 125 billion (the equivalent of $18.5 billion), compared with DA 1,880 million in 1978 and DA 408 million in 1973. Although the operating deficit of state-owned agricultural estates had fallen from DA 2 billion in 1980/1981 to DA 1.3 billion in 1983/1984, it remained high.

Most of the investments made during the period were limited in number, quality and geographical location. For example, in 7 years (1983–1987), only 27% of approved projects (5,186) were completed. Most of these investments were in sectors that were not very productive or job-creating. The trend was towards investment in the tourism sector (cafés, restaurants, hotels, etc.). Worse still, a large proportion of these investments were only made thanks to "links" established between private businessmen and the political staff in place. Most of the projects are often downstream from a state enterprise, the inner workings of which they are familiar with and where they still retain many links. Clearly, the emergence of this category marks a remarkable change in the sociological make-up of Algerian private business owners.

On the other hand, there has been a marked increase in the volume of investment devoted to housing, as well as the early payment of foreign debt. Housing accounted for 15% of total public investment, resulting in the construction of 400,000 homes between 1980 and 1984. The volume of foreign debt was reduced from $16.3 billion in 1982 to $12.7 billion in 1984. However, by deciding to focus development efforts on satisfying the social needs of the population, at a time when the productive capacities of the existing industrial and agricultural apparatus were largely insufficient, the State fuelled a demand that could only be met by imports. Obviously, these imports could not be sustained in the long term, as they were financed by oil revenues, which are an exogenous variable, dependent on fluctuations in the oil market. In fact, in the mid-1980s, international gas and oil prices fell sharply and durably, and the financial crisis set in, with its many and varied consequences.

3.3.3 The open crisis: 1986/1988

If the object of political economy is built on the principle of the scarcity of resources and their optimal allocation, it is important—for a better understanding of the economic contradictions of the Algerian State—to know that until the mid-1980s, Algeria never experienced financial constraints. On the contrary, the State's financial comfort grew steadily throughout the 1970s and early 1980s. Indeed, the share of oil taxation in the State's fiscal resources rose steadily from 31.5% in the period 1970–1973 to 63.3% in 1980, after having been only 12% between 1963 and 1966. This increase in oil taxation is certainly the expression of the fall in ordinary taxation caused by the poor performance of the productive sector, but it is above all due to the increase in the State's oil revenues. The nationalisation of hydrocarbons in 1971 and the two oil shocks of 1974 and 1979 led to a steady increase in foreign currency earnings for the State. In the minds of most Algerian leaders, the rise in prices and the oil windfall are virtually irreversible.

The "loose" budgetary management already observed during the 1970s was accentuated throughout the 1980–1984 five-year plan, in particular with the monetary injections following the organic and financial restructuring of public enterprises and other policies to encourage consumption, such as the anti-scarcity plan launched at the beginning of Ch. Ben Jedid's term of office. This situation, with a real sphere made up of production units that were mainly in deficit and a large and expansive monetary sphere, though with no productive counterpart, was only tenable thanks to the importance of oil revenues. In other words, the sudden fall in world oil prices in 1986 not only reduced the State's financial capacity, with all that this implied in terms of its impact on the national production system, but also placed the various factions making up the State power in an unprecedented situation, causing total disarray in the face of the accelerating deterioration in the socio-economic situation of the population. Let's take a closer look at the depth and diversity of the immediate consequences of the oil shocks, and their "hazardous" management by the public authorities.

As we pointed out earlier, the economic reorganisation implemented by the State as part of the 1980–1984 five-year plan did not make a significant contribution to the national production system. The organic and financial restructuring of public enterprises did not prevent their deficits from growing, and the reorganisation of the agricultural sector did not reduce the country's dependence on food. Oil revenues continued to account for 95% of Algeria's trade balance.

The social situation of the population did not improve significantly either. Apart from the increase in domestic consumption brought about by the anti-scarcity plan, the housing crisis, poor health cover and other social problems remained untouched, especially as the voluntarist demographic policy of the 1970s was beginning to show its effects. This is to emphasise that, contrary to what a number of studies and the official discourse suggest, the crisis in the Algerian economy did not begin with the oil shock of 1986. This crisis merely revealed and accentuated an already tense economic and social situation, and the public authorities did not seem to be unaware of this situation since the idea of reforming the national economy was put forward as early as the end of the 1970s.

Two phenomena occurred simultaneously in 1986, which had a profound impact on the Algerian economy: the fall in the price of hydrocarbons and the value of the dollar. After peaking at $40 a barrel in 1981, world oil prices fell sharply from 1985 onwards. During the winter of that year, crude oil prices fell to $30, but within a few months this trend accelerated, reaching the point of $10 a barrel in July 1986, before finally stabilising at $15 towards the last quarter of the year, marking a 45% drop compared with 1985. At the same time as the fall in hydrocarbon prices, the Algerian economy was affected by another phenomenon: the fall in the value of the dollar. In 1986, the dollar lost value against several currencies: 18% against the German mark and 21% against the yen.

The first consequences of this reduction in external means of payment were seen in the sharp fall in investment volumes and imports. The 1985–1989 five-year plan was abandoned and its investment programme revised downwards: in 1985–1986 alone, the volume of investment was reduced by 9% a year. On the other hand, productive investment fell by an average of 13% a year between 1987 and 1989, and overall investment was reduced by 7% in real terms over the same period. In turn, imports experienced a negative growth rate of –7.8% on average between 1985 and 1989 (–0.5 in 1985, –16.4 in 1986, –6.7 in 1988 and –2.2 in 1988). In addition, between 1986 and 1987, household and business supplies fell by 32.6%.

The consequences of these simultaneous falls in investment and imports, particularly of equipment, were particularly felt by the national production system. The deficit of state-owned companies, which was already high, worsened due to a lack of supplies of raw materials and other necessary equipment; their bank overdraft amounted to DA 42 billion on 31 December 1988. In order to maintain social peace and conceal the extent of the crisis from public opinion, the government resorted to a number of practices whose consequences were more serious than the evil they were supposed to curb. It cut back on imports of equipment rather than consumption, resorted to short-term borrowing, and even went so far as to "*offer suppliers oil for semolina.*"[4] The result was a slowdown in investment programmes and an increase in financial costs, further penalising already fragile businesses and having a negative impact on economic growth.

To make up the budget deficit, the authorities were also printing money, which had the mechanical effect of fuelling inflation, increasing deficits and eroding the purchasing power of fixed incomes. For their part, workers launched strikes in State-owned companies to express their dissatisfaction with the general deterioration in the socio-economic situation, but also, and above all, to refuse to be blamed for their companies' deficits. Managers, caught between pressure from workers and pressure from their supervisory bodies, which gave them no management autonomy, preferred to sit back and wait rather than take decisions that would involve them in a direct confrontation with the system's decision-makers and their various clients.

Between government action to "hide" the effects of the crisis, action by the various networks and interest groups, and action by managers and workers who—in the absence of institutional recognition of their right to manage in the case of the former, and to protest in the case of the latter—multiplied strikes of all kinds, a vicious circle was set in motion. The crisis was constantly feeding on its own consequences, leading thus to the total paralysis of the system, which manifested itself in the breakdown of macro-economic balances, the worsening of the budget deficit and that of the public sector, a dangerous increase in indebtedness, shortages, the development of the informal market, and so on. The combination of all these phenomena has led to a rise in the unemployment rate, a fall in purchasing power, etc. In short, the accelerated deterioration in the social situation of the population, with what this implies in terms of increased social discontent, has been expressed through a proliferation of urban riots and workers' strikes.

Added to this were the divisions between the various factions making up the political regime over the nature of the solutions to be brought to the crisis. In short, all the ingredients for an outbreak of popular unrest were present, and this is what happened on 5 October 1988.

3.4 The Attempt at Autonomous Adjustment (1989/1993)

Since the 1986 oil shock, there has been a widespread awareness of the danger posed by the dependence of the Algerian economy on energy rents. At the highest levels of government, the idea of economic reform gained credence and support. The installation of the reform team and the powers it was given were a clear sign of this.

Back in 1987, the team of reformers launched a reform project to give autonomy to public enterprises and the agricultural sector with a view to making them more profitable. This project was admittedly limited in scope due to the highly restrictive economic and institutional environment. But it nevertheless paved the way for the dismantling of the rentier mechanisms of the administered economy.

After the events of October, the reformers' project, initially limited to the strictly economic aspect, was transformed into a dual political and economic transition, the aim of which was to break with the single-party system and the administered economy. In concrete terms, this experiment led to a radical change in the political and administrative environment governing the country's economic activity.

In many respects, this experience is reminiscent of the peaceful transition to democracy and the market in the Central and Eastern European Countries (CEECs) after the collapse of the USSR and the fall of the Berlin Wall. As in Eastern Europe, the reformers sought to challenge the rentier mechanisms of the administered economy in order to allow the dynamics of accumulation to take hold. However, there was strong opposition to this approach, particularly from influential players in the Algerian political arena. The experiment came to a screeching halt when the government led by Mouloud Hamrouche collapsed in June 1991, 23 months after it had been installed.

Two years after the reformers' experiment was called into question, the Algerian state proved incapable of honouring its international commitments regarding the payment of its foreign debt. As a result, after a long period of hesitation, the government entered into negotiations with the international financial institutions, signed the first agreement to reschedule its foreign debt in April 1994 and accepted the implementation of a Structural Adjustment Plan (SAP) under the aegis of the IMF. This plan was to last four years.

3.4.1 The period of Mouloud Hamrouche's reformist government

The reform process of the team led by Mouloud Hamrouche, which began in 1987 but gained considerable momentum from 1989 onwards, was part of a global perspective based on the need to link economic and political reforms. This new approach proposed radical structural and institutional changes to restore the respective roles of the State and the market. The former would regulate, and the latter would create wealth. The reformers' project, therefore, revolved around the gradual disengagement of the State from the economic sphere on the one hand, and the redefinition and overhaul of regulatory instruments and institutions on the other. It was on the basis of this legal and institutional approach that the reformers sought to break the bureaucratic straitjacket that had stifled the Algerian economy for decades.

As far as its programme was concerned, the Hamrouche government, from its very first public statements, showed itself to be faithful to the analyses and recommendations of the team of reformers contained in the reform workbooks. It affirmed its determination to continue the effort by deepening the reforms in agriculture that began in 1987, and those relating to public economic enterprises in 1988. Better still, with the new Constitution no longer hampering the introduction of market regulation, the reformers attacked the monetary and financial mechanisms on which the whole logic of the administered economy was based.

A reading of the government's programme reveals that balancing public finances and fighting inflation through money and prices were short- and medium-term strategic objectives. In addition, the government wanted to further disengage the State from direct management of the economic sector, "demonopolise" foreign trade and encourage competition at all levels.

Indeed, it is clear from the reformers' documents and public statements that, in order to implement its programme, the government was counting on the commitment and participation of citizens through associations, socio-professional organisations and elected assemblies. This commitment to involving citizens and economic agents in the practical implementation of reforms was a strategic option in the reformers' approach.

To sum up, and for the sake of simplicity, we can outline the reformers' programme along three main lines: deepening the process of autonomising the economy from the administration, freeing monetary and financial power from government control, demonopolising foreign trade and encouraging domestic private enterprise and foreign investment.

3.4.2 The autonomy of the administration's economic field

As soon as it was installed, the reform government decided to speed up the transition to autonomy for public enterprises. The end of February 1990 was set as the final deadline for completing the process of autonomisation of all Economic Public Enterprises, whatever their financial situation. Automatic credit was banned once and for all, and banks, like public enterprises, were made subject to commercial rules. Appointments by central authorities (ministries, presidencies, heads of government, etc.)—through decrees—of the heads of economic administrations and public enterprises were abolished.

In addition, the government proceeded to revitalise the participation funds which had been set up, but were not operational, throughout the period of K. Merbah. They were relaunched, sometimes in a brutal manner, with the dismissal of several of their managers and their replacement by managers committed to the new reform.[5]

In addition, the reformers accelerated the transformation of the agricultural sector, supervising the technical teams set up for this purpose and the chambers of agriculture, which were henceforth invested by farmers through democratic elections. Economic policies were also placed under the authority of the judiciary: the administration, which had previously been the guardian of the economic sphere, now had only a support and a posteriori control function.

As regards labour relations, the government worked to replace the old wage relationship established by the Socialist Labour Management with another based on contract and negotiation between companies and trade unions. To this end, laws guaranteeing the right to strike and trade union pluralism were enacted, marking the end of the single, "official" representation of workers.

Among the measures aimed at freeing the economy from administrative control is the liberalisation of prices. Until the late 1980s, prices were set administratively. This pricing system produced rigidity in local supply while encouraging the growth of imports. It also prevented companies from developing through the search for profitable combinations, as prices were not generally remunerative.

In economic terms, the system of price subsidies totally disconnected the national market from the world market, all of which was crowned by the phenomena of shortages, the informal market and inflation. The system of administrative price-fixing was a powerful brake on the emancipation of the economy from administrative control. With the aim of freeing itself from the constraints of administrative price-fixing, the reforming government introduced partial price liberalisation in March 1990. The new pricing system consisted of two regimes: administered prices, itself made up of several categories depending on the product (guaranteed prices, capped prices, prices with capped margins, etc.) and free prices. However, despite its partial nature, price liberalisation was a step towards strengthening the regulation of the sphere of exchange by the market, which reduced the central government's stranglehold on the economy.

Moreover, the project to distance the administration from direct management did not only concern the economic sector. It extended to all public sectors, such as health, education, universities and social security. The reform went even further, proposing that user associations be represented on boards of directors, where appropriate. The same idea of the necessary empowerment of central government sectors can be found in virtually all of the government's reform initiatives.

3.4.3 Freeing monetary and financial authorities from administrative control

Because of its importance, we are paying particular attention to this measure. We have already mentioned that one of the important actions taken under the reign of H. Boumediene, alongside the nationalisations, was the subjection of monetary power to political power through the promulgation of the Supplementary Finance Act of 1965. Since that date, all monetary and financial instruments have been in the hands of the executive, represented by the Head of State. Banking institutions became centres for implementing decisions taken by the political authorities. The role of the Treasury was strengthened, and it became the main player in the country's monetary and financial system.

This unlimited use of money had led to structural and permanent inflation, which, on the one hand, eroded the purchasing power of fixed incomes while, on the other, provoking a massive transfer of value to the private sector. In addition, the unlimited institutional recourse to monetary issuance concealed, in the short and medium term, the shortcomings of the system and, as a result, prevented an objective assessment of the economic policies implemented. The history of the monetary and financial practices of the Algerian State is instructive in this respect: the abusive use of printing money caused the DA to lose several of its functions in the space of a few years, becoming nothing more than a unit of account whose value was only artificially maintained by the administrative fixing of the exchange rate.

The reformers had clearly stated their desire to break with the automatic recourse to printing money to make up the deficit of public enterprises. Consequently, they sought to put an end to the centralised allocation of financial resources and the "systematic boosting" of the Dinar's value through administrative manipulation of the exchange rate. With this in mind, the Law on Money and Credit (LMC) was enacted in April 1990. The guiding principle of this law was the separation of monetary power from political power. The means was to institutionalise the independence of the Bank of Algeria.[6]

By establishing the autonomy of the central bank, the CML aimed to introduce new rules on finance and money that were compatible with market mechanisms. It introduced a new approach to monetary policy, new prudential rules and a new mechanism for supervising banking activity. It was intended as a means of putting an end to the executive's budgetary excesses and as an instrument for the sound management of public finances. In this sense, the CML constituted a revolution in the monetary and financial "mores" of the Algerian State and represented a decisive turning point in the process of economic reforms underway.

The main implications of LMC 90–10 for monetary and banking matters can be presented as follows: the establishment of a single monetary authority, the creation of an independent banking supervisory authority, the re-establishment of a hierarchy in the banking system, the introduction of profitability and commercial logic in relations between banks and businesses, and finally, the autonomy of the monetary and banking spheres from the fiscal sphere.

3.4.4 The demonopolisation of foreign trade

In line with the system of centralised planning, Algeria had opted to monopolise foreign trade channels. Since 1970, state control over this sector has been total: imports and exports were the exclusive domain of state-owned companies. Foreign trade operations were strictly regulated and monitored by the public administration. The Global Import Authorisation (GIA) system was introduced, making all import operations subject to the approval of two ministries, Finance and Trade. From 1978 onwards, the system became even more complicated with the introduction of Law 78–02, which prohibited any intermediation between state-owned companies and their suppliers.

Other measures were taken as the State's external resources dwindled in the mid-1980s. In a last-ditch battle against rising imports, Prime Minister A. Brahimi set up an "external balances" committee. Brahimi set up the "External Balance" Committee, which he chaired several times a week, to monitor the conformity and "usefulness" of import operations. It is certainly not appropriate to recall here the many consequences, each as harmful as the next, at the head of which is the phenomenon of corruption through commissions on contracts.

The liberalisation of foreign trade was one of the most difficult areas of reform. Between 1988 and 1990, several attempts were made, including the law of July 1988, which stipulated that the State was not directly responsible for foreign trade, i.e., it had only granted concessions to public companies and organisations. However, for a number of reasons, the most important of which was the fact that the Constitution still indicated the socialist nature of the State, these measures did not bring about the necessary changes.

It was the Law on Money and Credit and the Supplementary Finance Law of 1990 that definitively broke the State monopoly on foreign trade. In accordance with the new legislation, the Bank of Algeria authorised the installation of foreign dealers and wholesalers. This action was all the more surprising given that the government had taken every precaution not to provoke criticism from conservatives—to safeguard the national interest. It imposed three conditions on dealers wishing to set up in Algeria: firstly, they had to cover the set-up costs by bringing in foreign currency from abroad; secondly, imports of goods for resale could only be made from the operator's foreign currency account; and thirdly, the operator had to undertake to promote investment in goods and services in Algeria on the basis of a set of specifications with a pre-established timetable—this was referred to at the time as "industrialising trade." In response to the lack of interest from foreign operators, the government promulgated another decree in February 1991, authorising any public or private operator to access the import market. The only condition maintained was that the operator had to have a bank account in Algeria.

The reform government's determination to put an end to the State monopoly on foreign trade is justified by the need to safeguard the national interest in the face of rentiers of all stripes who sell off the nation's wealth in the name of statism.

3.4.5 Uninhibited openness to the private sector and foreign capital

As soon as it took office, the reforming government put an end to the "historic misunderstandings" between the state and the private sector. It annulled all the laws hindering the exercise of industrial or commercial activity by private nationals: from now on, there would be no limits on obtaining a trade register or access to bank credit. Going even further, the government envisaged legalising part of the informal trade known as "*trabendo.*" But it is in the rules governing foreign investment that the reformist government has turned the planning system on its head.

After several decades of total mistrust of foreign capital, which was equated with imperialism, the government changed all the rules by introducing, within the framework of the LMC, the possibility for non-resident investors to set up in Algeria, either alone or in partnership with a local public or private company. Guarantees for the repatriation of capital and dividends were provided for in the law and in the international conventions that Algeria had just ratified.[7]

3.4.6 Political crisis, economic trial and outbreak of violence (1991–1993)

After the army's heavy-handed intervention in June 1991, the establishment of a state of siege and the "resignation" of the reformist government, the Algerian decision-makers formed a new government under the leadership of S.A. Ghozali. His official task was to prepare for the legislative elections scheduled for the end of December that year.

The government of S.A. Ghozali did not have an economic programme as such. Its term of office was set at six months, but it remained in office for a year. Gradually, the government of S.A. Ghozali departed from its original mission and devoted itself to calling into question most of the reform measures taken by its predecessor.

Indeed, despite its rhetoric on the need for reform, the government of S.A. Ghozali proceeded to systematically freeze most of the measures taken by its predecessor. Clearly, the mechanism of political concession to economic rigour was working again.

The consequences of this sudden shift in economic policy direction for the productive apparatus, particularly the public sector, were chaotic. Uncertainty, misunderstanding and, above all, the lack of clear economic objectives and plans brought the management system to a complete standstill. However, the freeze on reforms, the wait-and-see attitude and passivity did not prevent the economic situation from worsening, the social conditions of the population from deteriorating, and the foreign debt from mounting. Faced with these thorny problems, the government found a solution: a return to the blessed era of hydrocarbons. It declared before the National Assembly: "*If necessary, I am prepared to sell 20 to 25% of Hassi Messaoud and I will come back to you to do so. What is Hassi Messaoud compared to the future of my country? What use would this wealth be if I refrained from using it to save the national economy, to spare my people suffering and to safeguard their future?*"[8]. Once again, the "miracle" solution is resurfacing to avoid painful economic reforms: oil revenues and all that they imply in terms of ease of management.

Meanwhile, the first round of "clean and honest" legislative elections—the government's main task—took place on 27 December 1991, with the second round scheduled for 16 January 1992. The result gave the FIS the majority of seats, followed by the FFS and then the FLN[9]. Once again, the army intervened, annulling the elections and removing the President from office. After the economic coup against the reformers, the army staged a political coup against the results of the ballot box. Unprecedented violence was unleashed and continues to this day. Thus, the dual political and economic transition that began after the events of October ended in bloodshed.

When the democratic process came to a halt in 1992 and Ch. Ben Jedid was forced to resign, the country found itself in a virtual institutional vacuum, with no institutions in place. It was decided to create an institution from scratch—because it had never been provided for in the constitution—the High State Committee (HSC). This took the form of a collegiate presidential body made up of five members. It was initially chaired by Mohamed Boudiaf. A historic figure in the national movement, an opponent of the regime since 1962 and sentenced to death, he had fled Algeria and taken refuge in Morocco since 1963. He accepted this responsibility because he felt that the country was in danger. He was assassinated during a rally broadcast live on Algerian television on 29 June 1992.

When the mandate of S.A. Ghozali's government came to an end, he was replaced by B. Abdeslam at the beginning of July 1992. Thus, the history of the Ghozali government is associated with the total undermining of the dual transition to democracy and the market that began in the aftermath of the events of October 1988. It is also synonymous with serious political events that opened the door to a period of extreme violence that continues to this day.

The development of the political and security crisis and the assassination of Mohamed Boudiaf on 29 June 1992 were synonymous with the end of the economic and political transitions that had been abruptly interrupted in June 1991 and January 1992, respectively. Henceforth, it was no longer time for reforms but for "eradicating terrorism." Consequently, a "war economy" had to be established. The expression appealed to the military—it belonged to the new head of government, B. Abdeslam. He was Minister for Heavy Industry from 1965 to 1977. He was H. Boumediene's most trusted advisor in the field of economics. He was responsible for implementing the strategy of development through industrialisation. Being a statist, voluntarist and authoritarian, he did not believe in the scientific validity of economic laws. He believed that only the State was capable of leading the battle for development. He cultivated an extreme distrust of the private sector, which he described as parasitic.

Taking advantage of the general confusion at the top of the State, B. Abdeslam, once in power, wanted to turn back time. He declared war on the reforms initiated since 1980, in the name of the war economy. He returned to centralisation and economic dirigisme, (re)monopolised foreign trade, put an end to the independence of the Central Bank, and excluded the national private sector from public contracts… all that was missing was a large-scale nationalisation operation.[10]

Acting against the tide of history, the government of B. Abdeslam's government did not last long. He was dismissed in October 1993 under the combined pressure of mounting internal deficits and external pressure, particularly from Algeria's creditors and international financial institutions, which took a dim view of this twentieth-century statist. In July 1992, B. Abdeslam was replaced by a man with a completely different background and convictions, namely R. Malek. Once again, Algerian economic policy underwent a spectacular turnaround: from centralised economic dirigisme to structural adjustment. This fact reveals, in more ways than one, the political and economic culture of the senior hierarchy of the Algerian army, which has primary and ultimate responsibility for appointing and dismissing governments in times of emergency.

3.5 Conclusion

This chapter looks at Algeria's economic history under the system of centralised planning and its intelligent, but aborted, move towards a market economy.

The first section deals with the 1960s and 1970s. A period during which Algeria implemented what is known as the Algerian Development Strategy.

By its very name, it is clear that Algeria had a strategy, with all that this term implies. We described the mechanisms and dissected the operation and results of this strategy. The conclusion is clear: in relation to its initial objectives, it was a resounding failure. The SAD and/or its practical implementation have merely paved the way for specialisation within the international division of labour in the intensive exploitation of hydrocarbons.

The second section examines the nature of the measures taken by the successors to the powerful industrialists under H. Boumediene. These measures proved to be as ineffective as they were harmful. Ineffective because they were unable to rectify the shortcomings of the previous strategy, but also and above all harmful because they led to the gradual dismantling of the national industrial fabric inherited from the investments of the previous management team.

After the major financial repercussions of the 1986 oil crisis, some of the country's leaders were convinced of the need to radically reform the Algerian economy. To this end, a team of reformers was set up in 1987. This team was transformed into a government a few months after the tragic events of October 1988, which paved the way for a dual political and economic transition with the promulgation of the 1989 constitution.

The clear and resolute orientation of the reformist government towards dismantling the rentier mechanisms of the political and economic system aroused a number of oppositions, including that of the most powerful institutions, namely the powerful leaders of the army, which led to its downfall. Barely two years after the end of the democratic parenthesis of 1989, the country found itself in default of payment, hence the acceptance of a Structural Adjustment Plan under the aegis of the International Financial Institutions, led by the IMF.

The next chapter will be devoted to the analysis of two important periods in the history of independent Algeria: the first corresponds to the years of application of the Structural Adjustment Plan, the second to the twenty-first century. The second relates to the various post-Adjustment economic actions (the 2000s), a period during which the State enjoyed a financial opulence unprecedented in its contemporary history.

Notes

1 Charter and Order of 16. 11. 1976, on the Socialist Management of Enterprises, Ministry of Information, Algiers. 1972. This law can be consulted at: https://www.dgfp.gov.dz/texte/02.pdf

2 For the sources of the various statistics contained in this chapter, see, Ouchichi Mourad, (2011). L'obstacle politique aux réformes économiques en Algérie. Doctoral thesis in Political Science defended at L'Institut d'études politiques de Lyon II (France). The thesis is available on the website: https://www.theses.fr/2011LYO20067

3 For a detailed analysis of the conduct of monetary policy during this period, see, Ouchichi Mourad, (2011). L'obstacle politique aux réformes économiques en Algérie. Doctoral thesis in Political Science defended at L'Institut d'études

politiques de Lyon II (France). Part One, Chapter 2. https://theses.univ-lyon2.fr/documents/lyon2/2011/ouchichi_m

4 See the testimony of Gouméziane, S. (2004). Le Fils de Novembre, Témoignage pour le cinquantenaire du 1er novembre 1954, Paris-Méditerranée, Paris. 335 pp.

5 The Minister for the Economy, G. Hidouci made a statement of great significance. It provided information on the poisonous climate in which the transition was taking place: "Around thirty executives have moved, twenty of whom have been placed in other positions. I have the impression that in this affair, the politicians of the past would have us believe that we have destabilised the executives (..) in fact what bothers the politicians of the old system is that we have removed two or three executives who were strategic for them" in, Algérie-actualité of 27/12/1990 (Algerian daily newspaper).

6 We believe it is useful to briefly recall the historical background that first led Western societies, including the United Kingdom, to envisage the independence of the Central Bank. The onset of the industrial revolution brought about a profound socio-economic and political reorganisation within Western societies: previously favourable to social forces deriving their assets (and power) from the private appropriation of income (historically from agriculture), the balance of power has shifted in favour of social strata rooted in production. The latter—politically represented by the bourgeoisie— refused to allow the monetary value of the wealth produced by labour to be subordinated to "the mood of the prince." The emerging bourgeoisie could not tolerate the fact that the monetary value of its capital constantly fluctuated according to extra-economic circumstances. In other words, the owners of capital no longer wanted "the prince" to have the power to cream off the value of the wealth produced by a simple political decision. Consequently, the power to mint money had to be subject to a materiality that would put an end to the "monetary despotism of the prince." In other words, the assurance of convertibility and the stabilisation of "money flows" through the granting of metallic cover (cogs) to the currency had to protect the monetary rate from the "prince's deed." This is why the European bourgeoisie embarked on the struggle to impose the independence of the institution issuing the monetary counterpart to material wealth, in this case the issuing institution (the Central Bank). The Algerian development experience is very suggestive in this respect; it reminds us that when monetary power is totally subject to political power, the risk of seeing the money supply (and the value of the monetary unit) completely disconnected from the volume of goods and services actually produced is imminent. This is all the more true when the state has a source of income external to the local labour process, such as oil revenues.

7 See Bank of Algeria regulation 90/03 of 08/09/90. This legal text is available on the Bank of Algeria website https://www.bank-of-algeria.dz/wp-content/uploads/2023/01/reglement9003.pdf

8 Algérie actualité 22-28/08/1991. Algerian news daily

9 The final results of the first round of the 1991 legislative elections, as announced by the Constitutional Council on 30/12/91, were as follows: out of 13258454 registered voters, 6897719 votes were cast, i.e. just over 50%. The day after the first round, 231 of the 440 seats were filled, of which 188 went to the FIS, 25 to the FFS and 16 to the FLN.

10 The government is contesting the plan to give public companies autonomy and to manage them through holding funds. It intends to reorganise companies by branch and by industrial and financial groups under the direct supervision of the ministries, according to the government's programme (El-Moudjahid, 20/09/1992. Algerian daily accessible from the website: https://www.elmoudjahid.dz/). In the same vein, we cite the decision to reintroduce executive appointment of public sector managers; see article 117 of the 1993 Finance Act, which stipulates that "Notwithstanding any provisions to the contrary, on a transitional basis for a period of three years,

CEOs and chairmen of EPE DGs may exceptionally be appointed in this capacity or relieved of their duties by executive decree." In addition, the government promulgated Circular No. 4 of 11/10/1992 from the Ministry of the Interior to the walis, which instituted the exclusive award of public contracts in the construction and public works sector to State-owned companies only, even though private companies may prove more competitive. In the same vein, an executive decree ordered public companies and public administrations to entrust advertising resources exclusively to State-owned communications companies (Executive Decree of 09/08/93). This text of the law can be accessed on the website of the General Secretariat of the Algerian Government: https://www.joradp.dz/FTP/jo-francais/1993/F1993053.PDF). Ironically, this decree is still in force. It is regularly denounced by the national private press because the State's monopoly on advertising is often used to punish titles critical of executive decisions.

References

Addi, L. (1990). L'Impasse du populisme. Alger: OPU.

Brahimi, A. (1991). L'Economie algérienne. Alger: OPU.

Dahmani, A. (1999). L'Algérie à l'épreuve. Economie politique des réformes 1980-1997. L'Harmattan.

National Charter. (1976). *Journal officiel de la République algérienne démocratique et populaire* [Official Gazette of Algeria].

4 From structural adjustment to the transition freeze (1994–2023)

4.1 Introduction

With Mouloud Hamrouche's reformist government forced to resign, and after several months of political and economic procrastination (change of several governments, attempts to reactivate the administered economy, extension of the life of the HCE and the appointment of a military officer to head it, L. Zeroual, etc.), Algeria went into default and had to negotiate with the IMF. It agreed to reschedule its foreign debt in return for implementing the Structural Adjustment Plan. The IMF imposed its consensus, and the rivalries within the government between those in favour of openness and those in favour of the *status quo* ceased momentarily. But differences remained latent and resurfaced as soon as the country's financial situation improved.

The four-year PAS consisted of a series of reform measures with three objectives: macro-economic stabilisation, market liberalisation and, finally, the privatisation of loss-making state-owned companies; in short, the transformation of the centrally planned economy into a market economy.

The results of this new experiment in reform have been mixed. While the country has seen appreciable improvements in macroeconomic terms, the consequences in microeconomic terms have been disastrous: deindustrialisation, food dependency, unemployment, falling purchasing power, etc.

From 1998, when the Structural Adjustment Plan came to an end, Algeria entered a new phase in its history. The significant and sustained rise in international hydrocarbon prices provided the country with colossal financial resources. Taking advantage of this financial windfall, the government changed its strategy and approach. Instead of structural reforms to deepen the transition to a market economy, Algerian leaders preferred to invest in infrastructure through Keynesian-style economic recovery plans, as if the Algerian economy were not in structural crisis but in cyclical recession. This is the nonsense of the economic policy adopted by the Algerian authorities during the 2000s.

This chapter is therefore divided into two main sections: firstly, the highlights of these two eventful periods (1994–1998 and 1999–2023) and secondly,

DOI: 10.4324/9781003665571-5

an analysis of the ins and outs of the various players involved in implementing the actions undertaken. Finally, based on the data available to us, we will draw up a quantitative and qualitative assessment for each of these periods.

4.2 Adoption of the SAP (1994–1998): The second "failed" transition to the market

As soon as it was installed in October 1993, R. Malek's government distanced itself from the economic policy advocated by its two predecessors (S.A. Ghozali and B. Abdeslam). Barely six months after taking office, the government signed a "*stand-by* agreement" with the IMF, paving the way for the rescheduling of public and private external debt with the Paris and London Clubs. This so-called "stabilisation" agreement—the third since 1989—lasted a year, from May 1994 to April 1995. It was followed by another so-called extended financing agreement lasting 3 years, but more restrictive, as it included conditions that the IMF usually imposes on countries requesting rescheduling. The rescheduling of foreign debt, which had long been refused, was finally adopted on less favourable terms than in 1986 or 1991.

The agreement with the IMF was clearly not an option "chosen" by the government. It was imposed because of the deterioration in the country's economic, social and security situation. The much-anticipated improvement in world oil and gas prices failed to materialise—on the contrary, oil prices fell even further in 1993—and the patch-up policies adopted by successive governments worsened the situation. The result was the "forced composition" with the International Financial Institutions. The Structural Adjustment Plan became unavoidable. It was presented to Algerians as the only solution open to the country by the same actors who had previously demonised it for several years, in the name of safeguarding national sovereignty.

4.2.1 The conditions under which the SAP came into being in Algeria and its main results

The "forced" acceptance by the Algerian authorities of debt rescheduling and the Structural Adjustment Plan took place in an extremely tense political, economic and social context. Indeed, while the stoppage of the electoral process in 1992 plunged the country into increasingly extreme violence, the questioning of the economic and institutional reforms initiated in 1989 and the attempts to rehabilitate the administered economy only aggravated an already difficult situation, especially as the social conditions of the population were deteriorating at an accelerated rate. The public sector was at a standstill. Reforms were frozen, and public sector executives were content to carry out "minimal" day-to-day management, more specifically "managing" the payment of salaries and fulfilling the few orders received from the state or other public enterprises. Meanwhile, the structural constraints on the Algerian economy were worsening; the public deficit was widening,[1] the economy's dependence on hydrocarbons, food imports and foreign debt was worsening, while unemployment was rising. According to figures from the then Finance Minister, A. Benbitour (1998, p. 82), 95% of export earnings came from hydrocarbons, 75% of the calories consumed by Algerians were imported and the debt servicing ratio was 86% in 1993. On this last point, Algeria was in a situation of default. A simple arithmetical calculation shows that Algeria's annual revenue was estimated at $12 billion, of which the amount of $8 billion was for debt repayment, while the inavoidable needs of the domestic market were between $10 and $12 billion, giving a permanent annual deficit of between $6 and $8 billion.

In social terms, the situation was hardly glowing. Between 1985 and 1993, the working population grew by 1,980,000, while the number of jobs created did not exceed 800,000, further increasing the number of unemployed, estimated at 1,160,000 at the time.

Added to this were the effects of inflation, shortages and other phenomena such as the parallel economy and widespread corruption. The consumption index, to take just one example, rose from 10% in 1988 to 77% in 1993.

Politically, from 1992 onwards, Algeria experienced violence unprecedented in its history since the war of independence. Initially limited to the murder of law enforcement officers (police, gendarmes, etc.), the violence spread to economic infrastructures and civilians. Groups known as Islamists and other "unidentified" groups sprang up all over Algeria, spreading terror among the civilian population. These groups attacked the military, journalists, intellectuals and citizens, ransacking and destroying infrastructure and industrial equipment, and so on. Confusion reigned at all levels. In December 1992, the state introduced a curfew in seven *wilayas* around Algiers, with "no great" results. Entire regions were under the control of unidentified armed groups.

At the institutional level, none of the State's institutions were functional: the National People's Assembly (APN) was dissolved, the President of the Republic was compelled to resign, and the newly elected communal assemblies were also dissolved. The country functioned for three years without any constitutional political institution. The Presidency was replaced by the High Council of State, the National Assembly was replaced by a National Consultative Council (CNC) and then by a designated Transitional Council, and instead of mayors, the State appointed DECs (Délégués Exécutifs Communaux—Communal Executive Delegates). Political parties were marginalised, the press muzzled and the situation was entirely in the hands of the security services.

4.2.2 *The "Algerian" SAP between theory and practice*

As we pointed out earlier, the extended financing agreement, considered to be the real SAP, was preceded by a less binding agreement known as the "*stand-by*" *agreement.* This consisted of the implementation of an economic stabilisation programme, a necessary step before launching the actual reform process. To support this programme, the IMF granted Algeria a loan of $1.03 billion in May 1994. The broad outlines of this programme were based on three main points, which can be summarised as follows:

- Reducing the budget deficit and adopting a rigorous approach to monetary policy (reducing the money supply, stabilising the exchange rate, etc.);
- The devaluation of the Dinar: the IMF considered that the overvaluation of the local currency was one of the main causes of the trade imbalance in favour of imports;
- Liberalisation of foreign trade: the aim of this measure was to lift restrictions on imports and end the state monopoly on imports.

After a year of observation, the IMF and the Algerian authorities agreed to continue the SAP, leading to the signing of a second agreement on 22 May 1995. This new agreement led to a second rescheduling of Algeria's debt with the Paris Club in June 1995 and with the London Club in May and July 1996. It covered a total credit of approximately $1.8 billion under the Extended Fund Facility. This second agreement, known as "extended financing," should enable Algeria, after three years (in 1998), to complete its transition to the market. In other words, such a measure implies reducing its budget deficit, bringing its inflation and foreign debt under control, completely liberalising prices on its markets and all foreign trade operations, cleaning up its public sector and completing its privatisation programme. Algeria had already signed a debt rescheduling agreement with the Paris Club in 1994.

4.2.3 *Economic results and social consequences of the SAP*

Unlike the so-called "*stand-by*" agreements, the SAP is a reform programme with several components, ranging from the stabilisation of the country's financial situation to the total liberalisation of markets, including the privatisation of loss-making public enterprises. This is why it is wrong to reduce the analysis of the results of the SAP to macro-financial balances alone. In other words, to be complete, a study of the results of the SAP must look at the real economy and the social situation of the population. This is why we will present its effects according to three aspects: first, the macro-economic results of the adjustment; second, its impact on the real economy; and third, the social consequences.

4.2.3.1 The macroeconomic results of the SAP: Restoration of the nation's main accounts

Analysts agree that the macroeconomic results of the SAP are impressive, exceeding IMF forecasts. Indeed, after four years of "partial" application of the Plan, inflation has been brought under control, the exchange rate has stabilised and the state of public finances has improved. Finally, debt servicing is under control. For ease of reading, we will divide the macro-economic balance sheet of the SAP into three sections: the restoration of budgetary equilibrium, monetary equilibrium and those relating to foreign trade (balance of payments, trade balance, debt, etc.).

4.2.3.2 Restoring budgetary balance

A balanced budget was restored after 4 years of SAP implementation. After several years of deficits, the State managed to achieve a substantial budget surplus. This result was the fruit of an improvement in State revenues, but also and above all the outcome of a drastic reduction in expenditure.

The increase in government revenue was mainly due to the rise in international oil and gas prices. For its part, the reduction in public spending was due to the drastic fall in local purchasing power following the multiple devaluations of the Dinar and the increase in the price of imported goods. Figure 4.1, which shows budgetary resources, budgetary expenditure and the budgetary balance, perfectly summarises the origin of Algeria's macroeconomic performance.

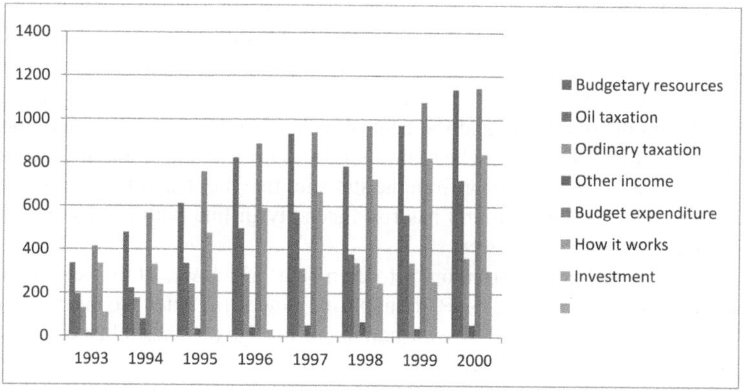

Figure 4.1 Evolution of budgetary balances (1994–2000). Diagram created by the Algerian Ministry of Finance (http://www.mf.gov.dz).

4.2.3.3 Restoring monetary equilibrium

One of the fundamental objectives of the SAP was to improve the monetary situation. In this respect, the IMF's goals have been achieved. The following tables, showing changes in the monetary situation and interest rates, illustrate the restrictive monetary policy adopted by the State. The fall in the money supply and the management of the various components of the interest rate indicate that the State adopted a policy of absorbing the money supply already in circulation. In this respect, it is easy to see that advances from the Central Bank to the Treasury have been reduced, the exchange rate corrected and prices are no longer subsidised, except for basic necessities. The fight against inflation became a credo of the State during the adjustment period.

A general trend in the second half of the 1990s was a fall in the rate of expansion of the money supply; the same was true for loans to the State and to the economy. The result of this restrictive monetary policy was to keep the inflation rate under control. After rising from 29.8% in 1994 and 34% in 1995, it fell to 5% in 1998. This was the most significant result of the monetary policy implemented during the Structural Adjustment Plan period. In addition, the exchange rate stabilised after the sharp depreciations recorded throughout the 1990s (5.9% in 1993; 77.8% in 1994; 21.6% in 1995; 7.7% in 1996, etc.).

4.2.3.4 Improving external balances

The combined effect of a strict fiscal policy and a restrictive monetary policy has led to an improvement in the external balance of the Algerian economy. Statistics relating to the evolution of the Algerian trade balance, the balance of payments, and the evolution of the stock of debt and its ratio between 1990 and 2000 show a definite improvement in the country's external balances.

An analysis of Figure 4.2 above clearly shows that the remarkable improvement in the balance of payments is a result of the improvement in the trade balance, which in turn is a result of the rise in international oil and gas prices, on the one hand, and the control of foreign debt servicing and ratios achieved through debt rescheduling, on the other. As far as the balance of trade is concerned, it is clear from the statistics that the share of hydrocarbons in the country's total exports has risen steadily in line with the increase in international crude oil prices.

With regard to the evolution of foreign debt, which was at the very origin of the application of the SAP, it should be noted that after having reached record peaks in the mid-1990s, the amount of foreign debt has fallen considerably as shown in Table 4.1.

This positive trend in external debt management illustrated in Figure 4.3 can be explained by a number of factors: first, the direct effects of rescheduling; second, the improvement in oil revenues, enabling the State to avoid

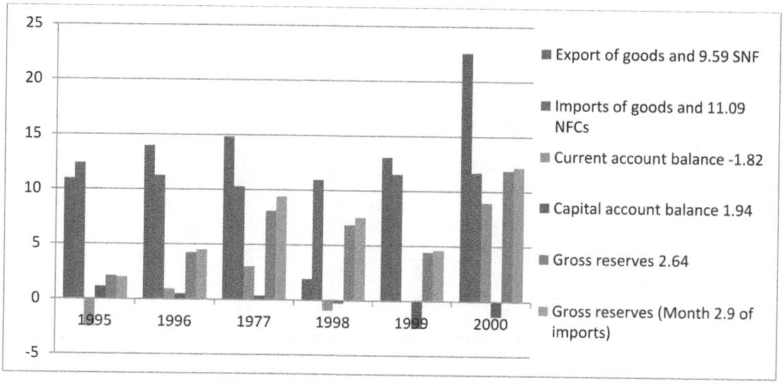

Figure 4.2 Algeria's balance of payments (1994–2000, USD billion). Diagram created by the Algerian Ministry of Finance (www.mf.gov.dz).

further indebtedness; and third, the reduction in the import bill resulting from the decline in domestic purchasing power due to the devaluation.

4.2.4 *The impact of the SAP on the real economy: A decline in local supply and an increase in extractivism*

In contrast to the macro-economic situation, the impact of the Structural Adjustment "reform" measures on the micro-economic level was at best unremarkable, if not harmful. In this respect, what is worth noting is the persistence, if not the increase, in the Algerian economy's dependence on hydrocarbons, the fall in production in the industrial and agricultural sectors,

Table 4.1 Change in debt stock and debt service ratio (1993–2000).

Years	*External debt (USD billions)*	*Debt service ratio (%)*
1990	29.80	69.00
1991	28.63	68.50
1992	27.08	76.60
1993	25.72	82.20
1994	29.65	47.10
1995	31.32	42.69
1996	32.09	31.48
1997	31.20	33.15
1998	30.20	47.80
1999	28.10	40.22
2000	21.36	21.23

Source: A table created by ourselves based on World Bank data and various CNES reports, 1996 and 1998.

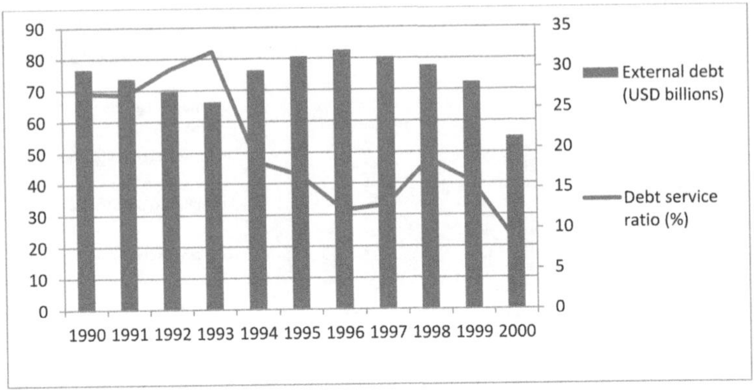

Figure 4.3 Change in debt stock and debt service ratio (1993–2000). Diagram created by ourselves from World Bank data and various CNES reports, 1996 and 1998.

the decline in factor productivity, etc. These are all factors which have had a negative impact on the Algerian economy.

With regard to the effects of the SAP on the productive system, it should be noted that despite its positive trend, GDP growth remained fragile, as it was essentially driven by hydrocarbon exports, as we have already pointed out in previous sections. Indeed, since 1977, the share of hydrocarbons in exports has exceeded 95% every year, and this rate has averaged 97% since 1998. Instead of boosting local supply to reduce dependence on rents, the SAP has, on the contrary, reinforced it in the name of specialisation according to the theory of comparative advantage, which, in Algeria's case, means intensifying the exploitation of its natural and mineral resources. The following Figure 4.4 on GDP growth by sector of activity largely confirms this already established observation.

These statistics show that, in terms of local supply and whatever the sector of activity, the decline is visible everywhere.

Adjustment's first victim was state-owned industry, which sank into a deep slump, to the point where it is no exaggeration to speak of de-industrialisation. In fact, during the 1990s, productive investment was halved to just 7% of GDP, resulting in a significant drop in the cumulative nominal growth of the industrial sector. The latter barely exceeded 6% between 1995 and 1998, which is less than cumulative inflation over the same period. This deterioration in the performance of the industrial sector can be explained by the same factors that led to the failure of the attempt at industrialisation in the 1970s: the under-utilisation of production capacity. According to R. Abdoune, capacity utilisation in the industrial sector fell from 57.2% in 1990 to 51.8% in 1993, and then to 48.5% and 46.7% in 1994 and 1995, respectively. Worse

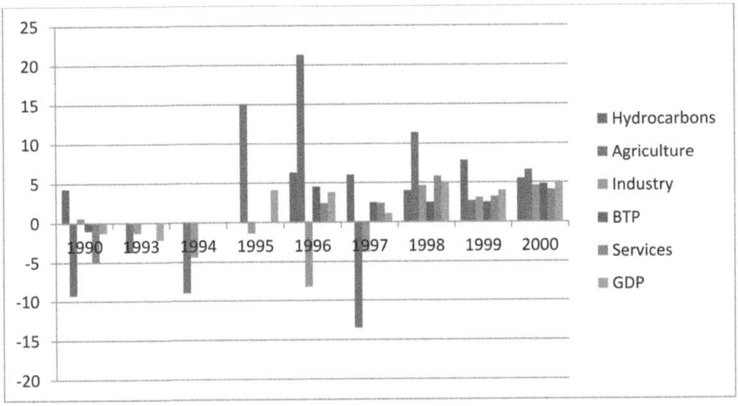

Figure 4.4 GDP growth in Algeria (1990–2000). Diagram created by World Bank, Economic Memorandum, 1993.

still, the net operating surpluses of state-owned industry have shrunk considerably (–22% for construction materials, –15.56% for the chemical industry, 267% for ISMME, which has gone from a surplus of 9 billion to a deficit of 16 billion). And even worse, some sectors saw their deficits worsen (+130% deficit for textiles/clothing and +178% deficit for leather and footwear). In short, the entire non-hydrocarbon industrial sector saw its net operating profits fall by 4% in nominal terms. Only the agri-food, wood and paper and miscellaneous industries managed to improve their net operating surpluses.

Growth in the agricultural sector has been erratic, rising from –1.3 in 1993 to –8.3 in 1996, before suddenly increasing by 4.6 in 1998. This random trend can be explained by Algerian agriculture's strong dependence on climatic conditions. As far as industry is concerned, in the space of four years, industrial production fell from 1.5% in 1992 to –8.6% in 1996. The same is true of the bank overdraft of public industries, which, after being only DA 10 billion in 1994, reached DA 94 billion at the end of 1995, rising to DA 109 billion in 1996, i.e. 54% of their turnover (Bouyacoub, 1997).

As far as the private sector is concerned, it should be noted that it has developed significantly compared with previous periods. In contrast to the public sector, it has gained market share in virtually all sectors. For example, between 1995 and 1998, the private sector increased its market share in construction materials by 109% to 18% of the value added produced, in textiles and clothing by 105% to 65.05% of the value added produced, and in leather and footwear by 95% to 48% of the value added produced. The private sector has also made a spectacular entry into the hydrocarbons sector, where it increased its turnover by 1172% between 1995 and 1998, from 2.2 billion dinars to 28 billion dinars, producing 4.40% of the sector's added value. But there is a point to be made here: the private sector dominating the hydrocarbons sector consisted mainly of subsidiaries of foreign firms, and the sector as a whole had for decades operated as a sphere independent of the rest of the economy. We cannot, therefore, conclude that the rise of the private sector in the hydrocarbons sector is solely the result of the incentives introduced under the SAP. We can assume that it was more a response to the desire of the public authorities to immediately increase the revenues of the State, which was facing a major crisis in its means of payment. Also, because of its specific nature (low job creation compared with the added value produced, the sale of the product extracted from the subsoil in its raw state, etc.), the development of the oil and gas sector has had little impact on other sectors of activity.

It should also be noted that, overall, the Algerian private sector was poorly rooted in the productive sectors. The data available indicate that the main sectors dominated by the private sector are services and public works, in which it produced value added of 88% and 68% respectively.

On the other hand, it should be noted that, despite its low share in the creation of total industrial added value (around 30%), the private sector outperformed the public sector in terms of cumulative net operating surpluses between 1995 and 1998. The latter increased from 21.3 billion dinars to 44.8 billion, while the public sector fell from 30.1 billion dinars to 28.6 billion. Is this performance by the private sector due to greater mastery of production combinations or to the nature of the chosen activities (sub-contracting, profitable niches and monopolies ensured by the complicity of the administration, resale of imported products in their original state, etc.)? To our knowledge, no study has been devoted to this subject.

In addition, the opening up of internal and external trade has led to a proliferation of traders and private operators specialising in imports.[2] In this respect, change has been very rapid. In 1995 alone, the number of trade registers issued rose by 15% for individuals and by 1118% for companies. By the end of 1996, there were some 25700 private importers, compared with just 300 public companies, with an estimated import volume of $10 billion. Non-hydrocarbon exports, which remained tragically low ($861 million), were 94% covered by private companies.

4.2.5 The social consequences of structural adjustment

In social terms, the effects of the SAP have been disastrous. The already fragile social strata have suffered the effects of price liberalisation, redundancies and, above all, the consequences of the revaluation of the purchasing power of fixed incomes.

In terms of employment, the period of the SAP was synonymous with a significant increase in the unemployment rate. In addition to the low level of job creation, the workforce was reduced by massive redundancies (between

400,000 and 500,000, depending on the source) following the closure of several local companies. As a result, Algeria had the highest unemployment rate in the Mediterranean (officially estimated at 27% in 2001, compared with 20% in Morocco and 16% in Tunisia).[3] This rate is even more alarming if two phenomena are taken into consideration: the first relates to youth unemployment, which, according to the ONS, has exceeded 40% in several regions, particularly the major cities. The second is unemployment among women, who, for many reasons, did not register with the labour offices, making it virtually impossible to assess.

In addition, since the implementation of the austere measures of the SAP, the population has suffered the effects of a fall in purchasing power. This is a direct consequence of the successive devaluations of the national currency. In this respect, it should be noted that the Algerian Dinar, the value of which has long been artificially maintained at a high level thanks to the administrative fixing of the exchange rate, has undergone a series of successive devaluations, as shown in the following Figure 4.5.

The consequence of these devaluations was a significant fall in the purchasing power of fixed incomes (2/3 of the population). Between 1986 and 1996, purchasing power fell by a factor of 2 to 5, from the top to the bottom of the income scale. Compared with Morocco, average purchasing power per capita has fallen sharply, from double in 1990 to 90%. In Tunisia, purchasing power fell from 150% to 50% over the same period.

The following Table 4.2, which combines the wage index, the price index and the fall in purchasing power, is very significant in this respect. The data in

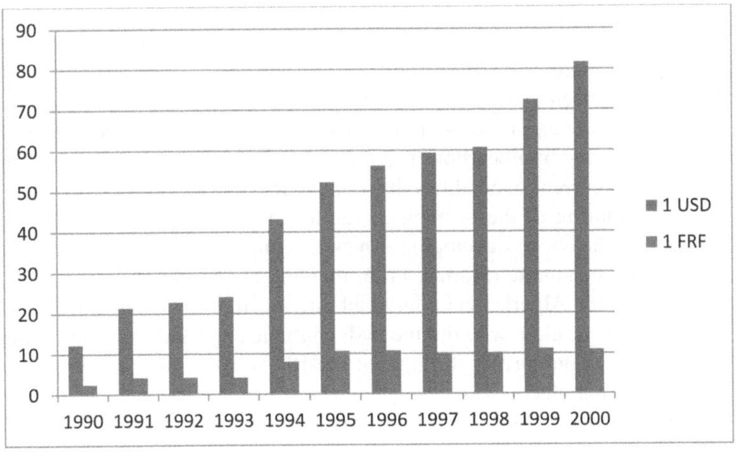

Figure 4.5 Dinar exchange rates (USD/DA and FRF/DA) between 1990 and 2000. Graph created by Bank of Algeria (http://www.bank-of-algeria.dz).

Table 4.2 Trends in wages, prices and average fall in purchasing power (1989–1995).

Executives	*Control*	*Execution*	*Total*
Index of change in average pay at end-1995 compared with 1989 (base: 100)	270	336	331
Index of change in the general index of Prices at end-1995 compared with 1989	442	442	442
Rate of fall in average purchasing power 41% in 1995 compared with 1989 (in%)	−36%	−20%	−20%

Source: A table by Bouyacoub (1997) in: "L'économie algérienne et le programme d'ajustement structurel," in Confluences, spring, p. 80.

the table below indicate that in six years (1989 to 1995), the purchasing power of employees fell by an average of 20%, and that of executives fell by around 41%. This situation is all the more significant when one considers that, until the mid-1990s, the proportion of wage earners in the Algerian population was high. The adjustment process has therefore also led to a social reshuffle in favour of the big traders, landowners and other rentier strata, to the detriment of the middle class and fixed-income earners in general.

In addition, the housing crisis has seriously worsened, partly because of the abandonment of the State's social policy, and partly because of the mass exodus of the population due to the security situation. Indeed, as a result of the terrorism affecting part of the population, more than a million people have moved from rural areas to the towns.

At the end of this brief presentation of the economic consequences of the SAP, at macro- and micro-economic levels, we deduce that since 1994, Algeria has engaged only in a deflationary stabilisation process, the price of which has been paid by the fixed-income and low-income populations. Price controls and margins on most goods and services have been abolished, and the dinar has been excessively devalued in order to guarantee the ability to repay the debt even in the event of a sharp fall in oil prices. The rise in the price of exported hydrocarbons (oil and gas), the halt in investment and the reduction in current expenditure have made it possible to avoid the necessary restructuring of the economy. Significantly, since 1998, the Algerian government has been developing a new discourse: that of the uselessness of structural economic reforms. From then on, the focus was on "recovery plans," as if the Algerian economy had only been in recession since 1986! This raises a question: why did the IMF continue to provide aid and support to the Algerian authorities throughout the 1990s, when its conditions were no longer being met?

Formulated otherwise, an analysis of the quantitative and qualitative results of the SAP, part of which was presented above, easily shows that the Algerian authorities have not complied with the IMF's conditions. With the exception of a few measures concerning money and credit, the structural reforms needed to move towards a productive economy have not been implemented, if at all. We are thinking in particular of market liberalisation and privatisation, which are fundamental components of the adjustment policies. And yet the IMF continued to express its satisfaction and support for the Algerian authorities throughout the 1990s. This raises the question of whether, in its assessments, the IMF took account of the country's political situation and tolerated the non-application of certain reforms that the authorities felt carried political risks. In other words, did the IMF make an exception for Algeria? There is every reason to believe so, since international financial institutions generally only take the economic aspect into consideration, whereas Algeria has not honoured all its commitments in this area.

By way of explanation for this situation, two hypotheses can be put forward; the first relates to the ability of States to "deceive" the vigilance of international financial institutions, while the second hypothesis calls into question the supposed total neutrality of international donors in their aid and adjustment policies.

The first hypothesis is that the IFIs do not have all the control capacities that are generally attributed to them. Firstly, at the theoretical level, the experts at the International Financial Institutions refer to the teachings of neo-classical and monetarist theories, which currently dominate the academic field of economic science, when drawing up SAPs and evaluating them. Developed in specific historical contexts, these theories are based on postulates whose relevance proves insufficient, if not completely meaningless, once transposed to market realities other than those of Western countries. As a result, structural adjustment plans are methodologically flawed from the outset.

In countries where the market sphere is not yet free of extra-economic interference (political, religious, moral), the concepts of price, effective demand and privatisation take on a completely different meaning. It is not enough to replace public monopolies with private monopolies to conclude that the privatisation process has been successful. Also, freeing up prices and devaluing the currency in a context of scarcity can only lead to a fall in effective demand without encouraging local supply. So, in the absence of consideration of all the parameters (economic, political, ideological, etc.) required for successful liberalisation, the IMF and World Bank experts are content to note the progress made on the legal front.

Furthermore, the way in which evaluation missions are carried out can also lead to numerous "errors" of assessment. They are carried out over a short period of time and exclusively within an official framework, which gives the States considerable leeway to manipulate the results of the application of the SAP.

Finally, it is worth highlighting the many collusions between international and national business circles, through governments and IFI experts. J. Stieglitz, based on his observations as Vice-President of the World Bank, delivers a scathing critique of the hijacking of economic reforms under SAPs by the business community to the detriment of the majority of the population, with the complicity of governments and certain IFI experts. He explains this by the weight of vested interests, but also by the failure of the institutional organisation of international economic relations. He argues for a radical reform of the current system, with greater citizen participation in the control of governments and international institutions.

The shortcomings listed above show that the organisation of the international monetary system allows governments a relatively wide margin for manoeuvre in order to "trick" them into applying the SAP.

The second hypothesis explains the gap between the IMF's conditions and the concrete implementation of the SAP by the strong presence of the political and ideological dimension in the relations between the IMF and its partners in financial difficulty. She points out that, contrary to what the discourse of the IMF and other international institutions suggests, the political and ideological dimension is often present in the decision-making of these institutions. The case of Yeltsin's Russia is often put forward to explain why, in the end, the IFIs grant favours to some countries and not to others, contrary to what their statutes state.

With regard to the Algerian case, we believe that the two hypotheses can be put forward simultaneously, i.e., that on the one hand there was a lack of vigilance on the part of the IFIs due to the Algerian authorities' ability to conceal information, but that on the other hand there was also a great deal of political influence in the way the IMF and Western countries handled the Algerian case.

4.3 Algerian transition put to the test by the State's financial opulence (1999–2023)

Since the end of the Structural Adjustment Plan, the Algerian state has adopted a contradictory attitude to the question of transition to the market. The rhetoric of economic reform has officially been maintained, but in practice, the state has returned to its dirigiste conception of the economy. As a result, the Algerian economy underwent a paradoxical evolution. Thus, the Algerian economy finds itself caught between several pincers, the most important of which are as follows: on the one hand, it was becoming highly centralised internally, but exposed to exacerbated external competition; on the other, it had substantial financial resources—hoarded in the form of idle foreign exchange reserves in foreign banks—but production in its industrial and agricultural sectors was in permanent decline. To summarise the situation, we could say that the Algerian economy is suffering from *mercantile syndrome, but without the protectionism that characterises it.* The results: a weakening of local supply, permissive budgetary and monetary policies, an explosion in imports and ever-increasing dependence on hydrocarbon exports.

4.3.1 A return to centralisation and economic dirigisme

Despite their imperfections, the various reform movements initiated during the 1990s opened up a significant gap in the administrative straitjacket that had stifled the Algerian economy for more than three decades. Paradoxical as it may seem, since 1999, the Algerian government has called into question the most important reform measures initiated during the previous decade.

Thus, after an initial disengagement from the economic sphere in the 1990s, the State is now being forcefully redeployed in the direct management of the public sector, completely reversing the relationship between the State and the economic and monetary sectors. Instead of contractual relations based on taxation and prudential rules governing the monetary sphere, we are witnessing direct interference by the State in the management and direction of the ebb and flow of wealth that is supposed to be regulated solely by the laws of the market. A study of recent government policies concerning the management of the economic and financial sectors largely confirms the assertion made above.

With regard to State management of the public economic sector, we have already emphasised that the objective sought by the reformers through the project of autonomy for public enterprises was to dissociate the State as owner from the State as manager. The creation of holding funds was a means of endowing public companies with a legal personality that would give managers the autonomy they needed to carry out their functions. In the wake of the Structural Adjustment Plan, the holding funds were replaced by holding companies with more extensive powers: the taboo of privatisation having been lifted, the holding companies could, for example, give their opinion on a partnership project with a foreign company, and even on the dissolution of "irrecoverable" public companies. Between 1996 and 1999, the holding companies even succeeded in signing a number of partnership agreements between state-owned economic enterprises and foreign companies, as well as dissolving a number of insolvent state-owned enterprises. Quite apart from the criticisms that may be levelled at the formula and the quality of the companies privatised, the holding companies succeeded in breaking the taboo on privatising the loss-making public sector, which had been kept alive by State subsidies since the 1970s. However, against all expectations, the State decided to put an end to this process.

In June 2000, the first attempt at centralisation was made. The 11 national public holding companies were regrouped into 5 holding companies, and a year later, the State repealed Ordinance 95–25 on the management of State market capital and privatisation. In August 2001, it promulgated Order 01–04 on the "organisation, management and privatisation of EPEs." Under this new arrangement, the CNPE became the Conseil de Participation de l'Etat (CPE), composed of 5 members chosen from among the ministers and chaired by the Head of Government, who appointed the State representatives to the boards of directors of the EPEs, determined the general privatisation policies and gave its approval to privatisation dossiers (Article 9). The holding companies were dissolved and replaced by 28 Sociétés de Gestion de Participations (SGP), responsible for managing the shares held in public companies on behalf of the State. Unlike the holding companies, however, the SGPs no longer have ownership rights over the capital they manage.

In addition, a Privatisation Control Commission and a Monitoring Committee were set up (Article 30). Under the new legislation, the privatisation process was further centralised, with the Minister for State Holdings and Investment assuming the role of central supervisor, responsible for drawing up privatisation strategies to be submitted to the Council of Ministers for approval. This extreme centralisation of the privatisation process, the withdrawal of owner status from the SGP, and the return of central government to direct management of the public sector, with the omnipresence of members of the executive in all the governing bodies of the EPEs, stand in stark contrast to the spirit of all the reform policies implemented since 1988.

As far as the State's relations with domestic and foreign private capital are concerned, it should be noted that after a relatively long period when the State seemed to have shaken off its historical mistrust of private initiative (various investment codes, various incentives, etc.), we have been witnessing for some years now the return in force of old reflexes blaming the private sector and foreign capital for all the dysfunctions of the national economy.

So instead of speeding up structural reforms and taking measures to encourage an increase in local supply—the only way to rebalance the balance of trade—the government decided to administratively squeeze local demand. To achieve this, four years after the Association Agreement came into force, the government promulgated and set out a battery of administrative and regulatory measures that were both contradictory and penalised the national production sector. These measures were mainly contained in the 2009 Supplementary Finance Act, the 2010 Finance Act and the 2010 Supplementary Finance Act. Against all expectations, the government decided in these laws to prohibit commercial banks from granting consumer credit, to require companies to pay for imports using documentary credit only, to introduce duty-free authorisation—a "disguised" return to the system of import visas—and finally, to require majority national shareholding in any private, public or mixed Algerian-foreign partnership investment project. These measures, presented as an appropriate means of reducing imports, in reality only serve to strengthen the grip of informal networks on foreign trade, while stifling the production companies still operating…

4.3.2 Challenging monetary power

We have already discussed the considerable advances made by the Law on Money and Credit of April 1990, which was intended to put an end to the subjection of monetary power to political power. The CML enshrined the autonomy of the Central Bank, elevating it to the status of a monetary authority free from political contingencies. Compared with previous laws, the CML is seen by many observers as revolutionary in terms of the way Algeria's monetary and financial sector is managed. However, this progress was radically undermined in 2001, when the Executive regained full management powers through monetary manipulation.

The nature and extent of the challenges to monetary power instituted by the State over the last decade will be better appreciated by comparing the CML with the 2001 and 2003 ordinances. While the CML transferred powers to the Conseil de la Monnaie et du Crédit (CMC), which replaced the executive in the area of banking and credit, the 2001 and 2003 ordinances reinstated the primacy of the government in the design and conduct of monetary policy.

In order to ensure that the Bank of Algeria had the necessary autonomy to exercise its monetary authority effectively, the CMA provided for a number of legal provisions, all of which were subsequently called into question. These provisions ensured the dual independence of the structures responsible for money and credit, both organically and functionally.

At the organic level, the Law of April 1990 introduced what is known as the "mandate technique," whereby the people in charge of managing the governing bodies of the Bank of Algeria and the CMC were protected from pressure from the executive. Article 22 of the CMA provided that the Governor of the Bank of Algeria and his deputy governors were appointed by presidential decree for a term of office during which they could be relieved of their duties only in the event of duly established incapacity or gross misconduct. The term of office, renewable only once, was 6 years for the governor and 5 years for the vice-governors. However, when the 2001 Ordinance amending the CML was promulgated, the concept of the term of office "immunising" the Governor of the Bank of Algeria and his deputies was abolished. Article 22 of the CML was repealed. The 2003 Ordinance, supplementing the 2001 Ordinance, confirmed this decision. As a result, the appointment of those responsible for managing the structures and institutions that are supposed to ensure the independence of the monetary authorities is now left to the discretion of the executive.

In addition to cancelling the principle of the term of office of CMC members, the 2001 and 2003 ordinances changed the composition of the CMC, increasing the number of government representatives. The CMC went from having 7 members, only 3 of whom were appointed by the government, to 10 members in 2001 and 9 in 2003. As a result of these amendments, the CMC was divided into two bodies: the Board of Directors, now made up of a Governor and three Vice-Governors, as well as three civil servants, and the CMC, made up of the members of the Board of Directors and 2 leading figures chosen for their expertise. This new organisation has reduced the number of representatives of the Bank of Algeria (4 instead of 5).

This questioning of monetary power at the organic level was repeated with regard to the internal operating rules of the bodies responsible for money and credit. It should be remembered that the CMA gave the monetary authorities broad powers, both for their internal operation and for their external prerogatives. For example, under the 1990 Act, the CMC was the only regulatory authority empowered by statute (not by executive decree) to establish its own internal rules of procedure. Also, in terms of the scope of the CMC's powers, article 63 of the aforementioned law (1990) stipulated that the CMC's decisions and regulations had the force of law, and the Ministry of Finance only had the right to appeal, which it had to do within a period not exceeding 10 days. In the event of a dispute, the Ministry's appeal for annulment was lodged with the administrative court. However, with the changes to the composition of the CMC introduced by the 2001 and 2003 ordinances, the CMC no longer has this power to legislate, in the sense that the government has more power to challenge the CMC's decisions. Firstly, the government can lodge an appeal, thereby triggering a second deliberation by the CMC. Secondly, as we pointed out earlier, the number of representatives of the executive is greater than the number of officials at the Bank of Algeria. As a result, the government can impose its choices during deliberations.

In addition, the banking sector, which should also have been subject to the rules of autonomy and commerciality, suffered the consequences of the State's dirigiste "neo-vocation," as did public economic enterprises. The process of modernising the Algerian banking system through liberalisation and inter-bank competition was brought to a halt by the public authorities. In the name of the prior recapitalisation of public banks, the State put an end to any hope of seeing the emergence of an autonomous, efficient and competitive banking sector. The same applied to the foreign exchange market, which the Bank of Algeria, under the impetus of the CML and the recommendations of the IMF, was beginning to promote by setting up instruments to allow the commercial convertibility of the Algerian Dinar through an interbank foreign exchange market – by promulgating regulations governing foreign exchange agents and the currency market.

After five decades of reform, Algeria still has no foreign exchange market. It is content with an interbank foreign exchange market, which is no more than a virtual space dependent on the Bank of Algeria, which has a monopoly on the currency and sets the parity on the basis of the State's political imperatives, not those of the economy. The value of the national currency, being set administratively, still does not reflect the real level of the country's economic and financial development. Like the decisions to call into question the principle of the autonomy of public economic enterprises and that of privatisation, the change in the regulations placing the Bank of Algeria under the authority of the Executive demonstrates a political will to reappropriate the management of monetary affairs, which led to the demise of the process of economic reforms previously undertaken.

But in contrast to this centralisation at the domestic level, since 2000 Algeria has been engaged in a sustained dismantling of tariff and non-tariff customs barriers, following the signing of the Association Agreement with the European Union. It has also opened up virtually all sectors to foreign investment, including telecommunications and air transport. This has not been without economic and social cost to the community.

4.3.3 Opening up to the outside world in all directions

After a long period of protectionism, the Algerian economy has opened up its foreign trade abruptly. In 2002, Algeria ratified an association agreement with the European Union, in 2009, it joined the Arab Free Trade Area and is now considering joining the WTO, thereby completely opening up its economy to international competition. All the signs are that accession to these various agreements poses imminent risks to what remains of the local productive fabric.

According to figures released by Algerian customs, the period 2001–2014 was marked by a surge in imports. This explosion in imports began in 2001, with growth peaking in 2004 (+46.7%), 2008 (+33.0%) and 2011 (+16.7%). Average annual growth in imports between 2001 and 2012 was around 33.7%.

Export growth, which soared between 2001 and 2014 with a growth rate of +287%, nevertheless recorded an average annual growth rate of +26%/year, 8 points lower than that recorded by imports. This growth in exports is, of course, driven by hydrocarbons.

Paradoxically, and in the face of this financial ease of the State thanks to the increase in revenues from hydrocarbon exports, the real economy has remained in a state of quasi-stagnation, with, in particular, a frank regression in the industrial sector. In 2012, the hydrocarbon sector continued to account for more than a third of GDP (37%), more than two-thirds of budget revenues (70%) and virtually all of the country's foreign currency earnings (97%). At the same time, industrial production remained weak compared with the extractive sector (hydrocarbons, minerals, etc.). This state of affairs is perfectly illustrated by the type of products imported.

In terms of imports, a breakdown by product group shows a general increase of 371.0% in imports between 2001 and 2014. The total value of imports rose from $9.9 billion to $58.33 billion. Non-food consumer goods recorded the highest growth rate at +579%, rising from $1.5 billion in 2001 to almost $10.0 billion in 2012. Capital goods (the second largest import item in 2012), including all categories of transport vehicles, rose by 284% between

2001 and 2012, from $3.6 billion to $13.8 billion. Intermediate consumer goods represented the 1st import item in 2012 with more than $14.0 billion, compared with $2.5 billion in 2001, an increase of 466%. Lastly, imported consumer food goods rose from $2.4 billion to almost $11.0 billion between 2001 and 2014.

Despite the facilities and advantages enjoyed by the private sector, such as taxation, bank loans and the introduction of the notorious 51/49 law on foreign investment (which has benefited the domestic private sector), these measures have not led to the emergence of a major industrial sector or an increase in the number of large economic enterprises. Indeed, according to figures provided by the Ministry of Small and Medium-sized Enterprises (SMEs), at the end of 2019, the overall population of SMEs is made up of 97% Very Small Enterprises (TPE) (workforce of less than ten employees), which remains highly dominant in the national economic fabric, followed by Small Enterprises (PE) with 2.6% and Medium Enterprises (ME) with 0.4% (Ministère de l'Industrie et des Mines, 2019). These figures indicate that the liberal economic guidelines that have been accelerating since the 2000s and the State's disengagement from the economic sphere in favour of private capital (domestic and foreign) have not had the expected results. On the contrary, the huge amounts of capital accumulated by employers—in the form of loans, tax exemptions and other benefits—have not been channelled into productive investment which has remained the poor relation overall; these investment projects have often been disguised operations to siphon off public funds, like the fiasco of the car assembly operation. In the end, the nagging promises to get the economic machine moving, to diversify the economy and to create economic prosperity—thanks to the creation of a class of entrepreneurs and an economy based on private property—did not last long. The proof is that as soon as hydrocarbon prices fell in 2014, Algeria went back to square one, just as it did in 1986.

At the end of 2014, a major event occurred with the turnaround in the oil market. The price per barrel fell from $96.29 in 2014 to $49.26 in 2015, then to $40.60 and $52.51 in 2016 and 2017, respectively, before rising slightly in 2018. Faced with falling revenues, the government panicked and took emergency measures, each as ineffective and harmful as the next. In addition to halting structural projects, the government decided to cut capital and operating budgets. The 2016 and 2017 Finance Acts cut the capital budget by 19% and 28% respectively. The cumulative budget cut is 41% compared with 2015.

Budgetary austerity was therefore set to become the order of the day. At the same time as wages were stagnating and public services were apparently deteriorating, thousands of civil service jobs were being cut on *the sly*. Indeed, after the abolition of early retirement, thousands of workers rushed to take advantage of this provision before it was abolished; only some of these workers were eventually replaced by new recruits. This phenomenon was mainly observed in national education and public health sectors already heavily affected by chronic attrition and a flagrant shortage of qualified staff.

However, against all expectations, this policy of austerity has been called into question since the advent of the *Hirak* and the rise in international hydrocarbon prices following the Russian-Ukrainian crisis. Once again, it is not economic objectives that are driving public policy, but political imperatives.

4.4 Conclusion

The implicit aim of this chapter was to compare the behaviour of the Algerian State during two diametrically opposed periods: the years of scarcity and the years of opulence. In fact, at the beginning of the 1990s, Algeria was in total financial asphyxia, and for much of the 1990s, without any economic sovereignty, given the IMF's conditionalities through the SAP programme. However, from 1998 onwards, the state coffers began to fill up at a significant and ever-increasing rate, following the substantial and lasting rise in international hydrocarbon prices.

An analysis of the economic practices of the state during these two periods, through the prism of the political will to make a successful transition to a productive market economy, leads to a conclusion which at first sight seems surprising: paradoxical as it may seem, the practices of the State remained the same; contrary to the official discourse advocating the need to reform the economy to make it productive through the market, the various governments fiddle with the laws of the market, prevent the autonomy of economic players, play with the value of the currency, block the emergence of a State governed by the rule of law… This leads to the growing computerisation of the economic sphere and the development of practices of corruption and predation at all levels of society. This is what we call a gradual shift from a rentier state to a rentier system. It is in this context that the discourse on renewable energies has emerged, hence the title of the following chapter: renewable energy development policies in Algeria: towards the reinforcement of rents?

Notes

1 The budget deficit reached 168.3 billion in 1993.
2 Companies specialising in "import-import," as popular humour has it. This expression is also used by the press.
3 The unemployment rate was 33% in 1998 (International Labour Office: www.laborsta.ilo.org/cgi-bin/brokerv8.exe).

References

Benbitour, A. (1998). L'Expérience algérienne de développement: 1962–1991, leçons pour l'Algérie au troisièm millénaire, défis et potentialités. Marinoor.

Bouyacoub, A. (Printemps 1997). L'économie algérienne et le programme d'ajustement structurel. Confluences Méditerranée.

Ministère de l'Industrie et des Mines. (2019). Bulletin d'information statistique des PME 2019. Ministère de l'Industrie et des Mines. https://www.industrie.gov.dz/wp-content/uploads/documents/bis/BIS-2019-11-35.pdf

5 Renewable energy development policies in Algeria

Towards the reinforcement of rents?

5.1 Introduction

In the previous chapters, we noted the strengthening of the umbilical link between rent and the Algerian economic sphere. This link is not a coincidence, but an objective result of the failure of the development project of the 1970s and the various reforms initiated since then, whether under centralised planning or the so-called market system. These repeated failures are the result of the nature of the relationship between the economy and politics in the country. In other words, it is the entrenchment of the economic sphere and the use of its resources to dominate society that is the main factor explaining the rentier and extractivist nature of the Algerian economy. The rentier and extractivist nature of the Algerian economy is evident not only at the macro-economic level and/or as a percentage of the State's foreign exchange earnings, but has invaded all aspects of the country's economic, political and social life to such an extent that it is more appropriate to move beyond the notion of the rentier State and replace it with the notion of the rentier system. In this context, to evoke an aspiration to transcend this system by promoting renewable energies seems to be, at best, an illusion and, at worst, simplistic rhetoric designed to satisfy an internal audience, since it is in line with the fashionable trend in developed countries.

Nevertheless, in a study of extractivism in Algeria, this subject cannot be avoided, as the country has undeniable potential in this area.

It is therefore important in this chapter to take a close look at the "efforts" made by the public authorities in this area, with particular emphasis on the country's energy assets: so what are the mechanisms and systems that Algeria has mobilised as part of its renewable energy development policies? To answer this question, we will first present the renewable energy development policy instruments used in Algeria, followed by the objectives of renewable energy development and, finally, the various renewable energy development programmes in Algeria, i.e., solar, wind, hydroelectric, geothermal, etc.

DOI: 10.4324/9781003665571-6

5.2 Renewable energy development policy instruments in Algeria

Algeria has mobilised several instruments as part of its renewable energy development policy. These instruments are based broadly on the legislative and regulatory framework, the creation of organisations (agencies, funds, etc.) and companies to support and accompany the use of renewable energies, and international cooperation in the field of new energies. In this section, we will look at the main levers of renewable energy development policies.

5.2.1 The institutional environment: The legislative and regulatory framework

The desire to promote renewable energies has led to the introduction of a legislative and regulatory framework to support the development of renewable energies. The development of renewable energies is governed by a series of legislative texts, namely: Law No. 99–09 of 28 July 1999 on energy management; Law No. 02–01 of 5 February 2002 on electricity and the public distribution of piped gas; Law No. 04–09 of 14 August 2004 on the promotion of renewable energies as part of sustainable development.

The purpose of Law 99–09 is to define the conditions and means for framing and implementing the national energy management policy. This law sets out all the measures to be implemented with a view to the rational use of energy, the development of renewable energies and the reduction of the impact of the energy system on the environment (Article 2 of Law 99–09).

However, the most important piece of legislation concerning the production of electricity from renewable sources is Law 02–01 of 5 February 2002 on electricity and gas distribution through pipelines. This law established the legislative framework for electricity generation in the application of the reforms to the Algerian electricity system. These provisions apply to all branches of production, including those producing electricity from renewable sources.

In this law, the legislator has provided for specific clauses to remedy the problem of the competitiveness of renewable electricity by instituting the support method deemed most consistent with the Algerian context. The support method chosen is the invitation to tender. In applying the energy policy measures, the regulatory commission may take organisational measures to ensure the normal flow on the market at a minimum price for a minimum volume of electricity produced from renewable energy sources or the cogeneration system.

The additional costs resulting from these measures may be subsidised by the State and/or taken into account by the electricity and gas fund and deducted from tariffs. The quantities of energy to be sold on the market and aimed at encouraging renewable energies or cogeneration must be the subject of a call for tenders defined by regulation. This quantity of electricity produced from renewable sources therefore benefits from a special regime. This special regime is set out in the draft executive decree on the costs of diversifying electricity generation, which was adopted by the Government Council on 28 January 2004.

Under Article 26, electrical energy produced by cogeneration systems enjoys the same status as renewable electricity. The concept of diversification costs is introduced by Article 95 of the law. Diversification costs are the extra costs inherent in a technological choice to use renewable energies. Producers may receive premiums to compensate for these costs. This designation of diversification costs is the expression of an important option in Algerian energy policy: the need to diversify primary energy sources.

Finally, the last piece of legislation relating to renewable energy is Law 04–09 on the promotion of renewable energies as part of sustainable development. Following the same logic as the previous law, the purpose of Law 04–09 is to set out the procedures for promoting renewable energies as part of sustainable development. Stambouli (2011) reports that during the period 2004–2005, the State took considerable steps to support the national energy efficiency strategy. This period will see the emergence of a sectoral energy network that will form the basis of the partnerships needed by the National Energy Directorate.

5.2.2 The Institutions involved in the development of renewable energies

The public players operating in the field of renewable energies are diverse and varied in terms of both their institutional importance and their areas of intervention. In addition to the Ministry of Energy, Algeria has mobilised organisations, funds and programmes aimed at developing renewable energies.

The Commission for Electricity and Gas Regulation (CREG) is one of the players involved in implementing energy policy. In addition to its role of ensuring that the electricity market operates competitively and transparently, its fundamental role is to ensure the organisation and operation of the renewable electricity market (Law 02–01 on electricity and gas distribution through pipelines).

The Algerian National Agency for the Promotion and Rationalisation of Energy Use (APRUE)[1] is the central element in the implementation of the National Energy Efficiency Programme. This agency is considered to be the national coordinator of energy efficiency policy. It is also responsible for providing information, communication and management training to all public players involved in energy efficiency. It is also responsible for setting up partnerships to develop cross-sectoral or sectoral action programmes within the framework of the PNME (Decree 21–106).

Approved by the Minister of Energy and Mines, the APRUE's energy efficiency action plan is part of the implementation of the national energy efficiency strategy, and its main mission is to encourage and support the initiatives of the various players and assist them in their efforts. In this programme of activities, the APRUE's main missions are broken down into sectoral objectives (national coordination, industry, residential, tertiary, transport, renewable energies, etc.) and associated actions (Decree 21–106).

The National Fund for Energy Management, Renewable Energies and Cogeneration (FNME) was set up in 2000 (Executive Decree 20–285) to finance energy efficiency investment projects by granting non-interest-bearing loans and guarantees on loans taken out with banks and financial institutions. It provides up to 70% subsidies for feasibility studies that contribute to improving energy efficiency in industrial companies. The aim is to encourage local products and provide advantageous conditions, particularly tax conditions, for investors wishing to become involved in the various renewable energy sectors (Executive Decree 20–285).

The FNME's annual budget is estimated at DA500 million (€57 million). The fund's resources include taxes on natural gas (0.00015 DA/btu) and electricity (0.02 DA/kWh), and an initial state contribution of 100 million DA (1.15 million euros). Additional resources may include taxes on energy-intensive equipment, penalties, loan repayments and government or other contributions[2] (World Bank 2009; quoted in Stambouli, 2011, p. 1180).

Created in 2019, the Commission for Renewable Energy and Energy Efficiency (CEREFE) is responsible for designing the national strategy for renewable energy and energy efficiency. It is also responsible for evaluating national policy in this area, the tools used to implement it and their impact (Article 5 of Executive Decree 21–95).[3] Algeria also has a national observatory for the promotion of renewable energies, responsible for promoting and developing the use of renewable energies (Law 04–09, Article 17).

Finally, this desire to promote renewable energies has also led to the creation of specialised agencies to promote research and development in the field of renewable energies.[4] According to the Ministry of Energy and Mines (MEM), three bodies in the higher education and scientific research sector have been in operation since 1998: the Renewable Energy Development Centre (CDER), the Solar Equipment Development Unit (UDES) and the Silicon Technology Development Unit (UDTS).

5.2.3 Economic players involved in renewable energy development

Algeria has involved the private sector in the development of investment, technology acquisition, know-how and access to foreign markets in the field of renewable energy. In this context, through public policies, Algeria has encouraged the creation of Small and Medium-Sized Enterprises (SMEs) specialising in equipment installation and maintenance, engineering, studies and consultancy. However, Algeria has relied much more heavily on the public

Table 5.1 NEAL's renewable energy production targets.

Requirements	*Local (MW)*	*Export (MW)*	*Total (MW)*
2000	500	75	575
2015	1000	400	1400
2050	1500	6000	7500

Source: A table by NEAL (2015).

sector to develop new sources of renewable energy through the two public companies known as Sonatrach[5] (Société Nationale des Hydrocarbures, Recherche, Production, Transport, Transformation et Commercialisation) and Sonelgaz[6] (Société Nationale de l'Electricité et du Gaz), which are responsible for investment in renewable energies.

Algeria has also relied on public-private cooperation to support the development of renewable energies. In July 2002, Sonatrach, Sonelgaz and the private company SIM set up a joint venture, New Energy Algeria (NEAL), to pursue the development of alternative sources of electricity, namely solar, wind and biomass. NEAL **is** the first public-private partnership. Its share capital of 200 million Algerian Dinars (AD) is shared between SONATRACH (45%), SONELGAZ (45%) and the SIM group (10%).

NEAL is a company specialising in the production of energy from renewable sources. Its field of activity covers solar thermal, solar photovoltaic, wind, geothermal and biomass. The company also promotes LPG (Bupro) to combat deforestation in the south of the country. NEAL's objectives are focused on increasing renewable energy production to 1,400 MW by 2030 and 7,500 MW by 2050. Electrical energy will be obtained from solar power plants that are exclusively solar, or hybrid solar power plants that use other forms of renewable or conventional energy, such as natural gas (Table 5.1).

To pursue the development of alternative sources of electricity, New Energy Algeria (NEAL) has joined the Solar PACES programme of the International Energy Agency (IEA). To carry out its activities, NEAL has sought several sources of funding and support for its projects. NEAL receives public funding from Algerian public institutions, in particular the Ministry of Energy and Mines. In addition, in order to benefit from aid from the World Bank, the International Energy Agency (IEA) and the European Investment Bank, NEAL has registered its investment projects within the framework of actions supported and financed by these international organisations (Stambouli, 2011).

5.2.4 International cooperation in the field of renewable energy

International cooperation is one of the levers Algeria is using to promote the use of renewable energies. Agreements have been signed between Algeria and countries such as Japan, Germany and Spain to facilitate cooperation in the energy sector between foreign companies, the Algerian Ministry of Energy and Mines and Algerian companies. According to the Ministry of Energy, these agreements emphasise the involvement of Algerian companies (joint ventures, joint ventures, etc.) with a view to facilitating the transfer of technology that can be used in the energy sector.

In order to benefit from international expertise and know-how, the Algerian National Agency for the Promotion and Rationalisation of Energy Use (APRUE) has opted for international cooperation relations. By acquiring a stake in MEDENER, the Association of Mediterranean Energy Efficiency Agencies, the APRUE will be able to keep abreast of the region's programmes, projects and actions. It will also be able to make itself known to funding agencies and promote both the Algerian energy efficiency market and energy policy at the international level. On a bilateral level, the APRUE has developed projects with France and Spain in particular (Stambouli, 2011).

In 2003, Algeria ratified an energy cooperation agreement with France. This cooperation agreement involved, on the Algerian side, the Algerian National Agency for the Promotion and Rationalisation of Energy Use (APRUE) and, on the French side, the Agency for the Environment and Energy Management (ADEME). Cooperation with Spain has focused on the energy-related industry and road transport. At the multilateral level, the APRUE has received grants from the European Commission, via the World Bank and the UNDP, for projects in several sectors. The APRUE intends to develop its international cooperation relations. Negotiations are underway with its Italian and Quebec partners, GTZ and UNESCO, with a view to developing energy efficiency projects (Stambouli, 2011).

In 1992, Algeria signed the United Nations Framework Convention on Climate Change (UNFCCC) following the summit held in Rio de Janeiro. In 1997, the countries that signed this convention (UNFCCC) accepted the Kyoto Protocol and undertook to reduce their GHG emissions to at least 5% below their average 1990 levels by 2008–2012 (see Table 5.2). (GHG emissions must not exceed 39 million tonnes in 2008–2012) (Himri et al., 2009).

Table 5.2 Production, Consumption and Emission in Algeria and Arab Countries.

	Power generation[a]			*Energy consumption*[a]			*CO_2 emissions*[b]		
Year	*1980*	*1999*	*2004*	*1980*	*1999*	*2004*	*1980*	*1999*	*2004*
Algeria	2.8	6.06	10.03	0.8	1.31	6.21	16.44	32.42	28.60
Arab region	46,82	55,57	62,54	6.27	13.59	21.48	268.40	268.40	354.21

Source: A table by Himri et al. (2009).

[a] Quadrillion (10^{15}) British thermal unit (1055.54 J).

[b] Millions of metric tonnes.

In 2010, on the basis of cooperation with the European Community, Algeria set itself the target of generating 10–12% of its energy consumption from renewable energy sources (7% from electricity) (Hassselager, 2003; cited by Himri et al., 2009, p. 911). By 2030, Algeria aims to produce 20% of its electricity from renewable sources, including 70% from CSP, 20% from photovoltaics (PV) and 10% from wind power. The country's strategy to develop renewable energy sources and implement a low-carbon economy fully supports its efforts to reduce vulnerability to oil prices and hydrocarbon exports. Algeria intends to become a leading nation in the renewable energy sector, including component manufacturing, thanks to abundant domestic resources and targeted policies (Stambouli, 2011).

Algeria is a member of the African Energy Commission (AFREC), an agency of the African Union (AU), placed under the Department of Infrastructure and Energy and responsible for the coordination, harmonisation, protection, conservation, development, rational exploitation and marketing of energy.

For the year 2023, AFREC has drawn up a series of draft energy programmes focusing on energy transition, bioenergy development, energy efficiency, capacity building and the African Energy Information System (African Energy Commission, 2023).

In order to benefit from international experience, the African Energy Commission (AFREC) collaborates with national and local governments, continental energy organisations, United Nations specialised agencies (the International Energy Agency (IEA), the European Union (EU), the EUREC Agency, the World Wind Energy Association (WWEA) and the World Bank (WB) and the International Solar Energy Society (ISES). The African Energy Commission (AFREC) also collaborates with local communities, Non-Governmental Organisations (NGOs), research institutes and universities (African Energy Commission, 2023).

To carry out its functions, AFREC relies on the Programmes for the Sustainable Development of Energy, the sponsorship of continental strategies and policies, the mobilisation of African organisations dealing with energy, the mobilisation of African regulatory and legislative instructions, the popularisation of energy management and the creation of the African Renewable Energy Society (ARES) (African Energy Commission, 2023).

Through these actions aimed at a sustainable Africa, AFREC aspires to the use of renewable energies throughout the continent, through appropriate technology, scientific excellence, social responsibility and continental communication, bringing together industrialists, individuals and institutions to support renewable energy technologies, through communication, cooperation, support and exchanges, applying practical projects, transfer technology, education, training and support African energy development issues, support renewable energy technology sciences, stimulate and encourage basic and applied research in renewable energy technologies, ensure rapid access to information through communication and exchange platforms designed on the basis of modern technologies (African Energy Commission, 2023).

5.2.5 Other policy levers for the development of new energies in Algeria

The introduction of a specific and competitive energy tax system (for renewable energies), combined with the formulation of more attractive investment conditions, will give new impetus to the development of activities in the energy sector. Interest in the development of renewable energies in Algeria has also been reflected in the development of awareness-raising and outreach initiatives to promote these new energy sources (Stambouli, 2011).

It is now important to inform the public and introduce special energy legislation to increase the use of this clean form of energy, in both the private and public sectors, and to demonstrate the importance of energy efficiency and conservation. Solar and wind energy are Algeria's most abundant natural resources. It is therefore imperative for Algeria to exploit this important energy resource.

5.3 Development objectives for renewable energy in Algeria

The development of renewable energies in Algeria meets a number of objectives, including supplying isolated and remote areas with energy services, preserving hydrocarbon reserves and mobilising the Clean Development Mechanism (CDM).

5.3.1 Providing energy services to isolated and remote areas

One of the objectives set by the Ministry of Energy and Mines for the development of renewable energies in Algeria is to provide energy services to isolated areas that are far from traditional electricity distribution networks.

Looking at the figures from the Ministry of Energy and Mines, the share of renewable energies in the national energy balance remains insignificant (18 villages electrified using PV in the south and Telecom Relays). According to Stambouli (2011), this situation cannot remain at an embryonic stage, and the interest in introducing renewable energies in Algeria is becoming a clear commitment on the part of the public authorities. The results of the proposed actions will make it possible to provide elements of assessment and decision-making support for the players involved in energy policy.

5.3.2 Preserving hydrocarbon reserves by exploiting renewable energy resources

According to the **Ministry of Energy and Mines**, the development of renewable energies in Algeria meets the objective of helping to **preserve hydrocarbon reserves** by exploiting renewable energy resources, particularly solar energy. The large-scale exploitation of solar energy to produce electricity connected to the grid will help to meet national needs and will eventually find an export outlet to European countries. This prospect is part of a sustainable development process that will help with the preservation of the environment. The programmes have included various solar applications: rural electrification, photovoltaic pumping, water heating and other industrial applications (Algeria's commitment to its national rural electrification programme, which continues to provide solar energy to villages in southern Algeria, after a successful first phase, the second phase is now underway).

In line with the **policy of developing natural gas,** a project to export electricity to Europe from a 2,000 MW power station is being implemented as part of an international partnership. Another of Algeria's objectives is to help preserve hydrocarbon reserves by exploiting renewable energy resources, particularly solar energy. Large-scale exploitation of the solar field to produce electricity connected to the framework will help to meet national needs and will eventually find an export outlet to European countries.

5.3.3 Clean Development Mechanism (CDM)

With the expansion of the energy and mining sector and the widespread availability of energy products for the population and industry, considerable efforts are needed to prevent damage to the environment and to the quality of life in general. The Energy and Mining sector attaches great importance to issues relating to the protection of the environment and public health. The integration of these concerns into sectoral policy is based on the "energy and mining policy" section of the government programme. This has resulted in the introduction of measures essentially linked to the following objectives: the promotion and development of the use of less polluting fossil fuels (natural gas, LPG, unleaded petrol); the promotion of energy saving; the rehabilitation of polluted sites; the development of renewable energies and the development of environmental management in the Energy and Mining sector.

The energy reform sector currently being implemented attaches great importance to the environment, with specific provisions introduced by the new laws on mining and electricity production. Environmental impact studies, the implementation of environmental management plans and the auditing of environmental complexes have been made compulsory by the sector and are also under its responsibility.

The integration of environmental protection and sustainable development into policy formulation, planning and management is an imperative for the sector, given the need to protect natural habitats, public health and also the country's commitment to international legal instruments and the various agreements and conventions concluded in the country. The main emitters of greenhouse gases (GHGs) are fuel combustion in the energy sector, industry and the transport sector. Other major contributors are agriculture, small-scale combustion, non-combustion emissions in industry and waste. The structure of Algeria's primary energy supply is very favourable in terms of greenhouse gas (GHG) emissions. GHG emissions in Algeria amount to around 84 million tonnes (fourth in the Arab world) (Stambouli, 2011).

The gas from the Ain-Salah field has a high concentration of CO_2, which must be reduced to meet pipeline specifications. After withdrawal, instead of being released into the atmosphere, the CO_2 is reinjected into an aquifer that is part of the same geological formation as the gas field. Today, the Ain-Salah gas plant is in full operation. The CO_2 produced from the natural gas stream is extracted in the desert processing plant and sequestered in underground storage. Sonatrach, British Petroleum and STATOIL are closely monitoring the performance of this major operation. The same firms are also developing the Ain-Amenas gas condensate field near the Libyan border (Stambouli, 2011).

5.3.4 Energy outlook and overall planning

In addition to providing a better response to future energy demand, energy forecasts can lead to proposals for energy policy measures that are best suited to the objectives of the decision-makers in charge of the energy sector. Obviously, energy forecasting is based on data and indicators concerning the current energy system, but also on information that may foreshadow a future change in the determinants of supply or demand. In order to define objectives and draw up an energy efficiency action programme, it is first necessary to have a clear picture of the economic situation in general and the energy situation in particular. The APRUE will carry out a foresight exercise in order to draw up the short-term action programme based on clearly identified issues. It is important to maintain this activity and to strengthen national expertise on the subject. In fact, it is within this framework that the reference framework for future energy efficiency programmes will be established.

5.4 Renewable energy development programmes in Algeria

In this section, we will look at efforts to develop renewable energies in Algeria. We will look at the mechanisms for developing solar energy, wind power, geothermal energy, etc.

5.4.1 Developing solar energy: Creating solar power stations

According to the Centre for the Development of Renewable Energy (CDER), the insolation time[7] over the national territory exceeds 2000 h annually and can reach 3900 h (high plains and Sahara). The daily energy obtained on a horizontal surface of 1 m^2 is 5 kWh over most of the national territory, i.e. approximately 1700 $kWh/m^2/year$ for the North and 2263 $kWh/m^2/year$ for the South of the country (Table 5.3 and Figure 5.1).

Table 5.3 Algeria's solar potential.

Regions	*Coastal region*	*High plateaux*	*Sahara*
Surface area (%)	4	10	86
Average sunshine duration (hours/year)	2650	3000	3500

Source: A table created by the Ministry of Hydrocarbons and Mines (2016).

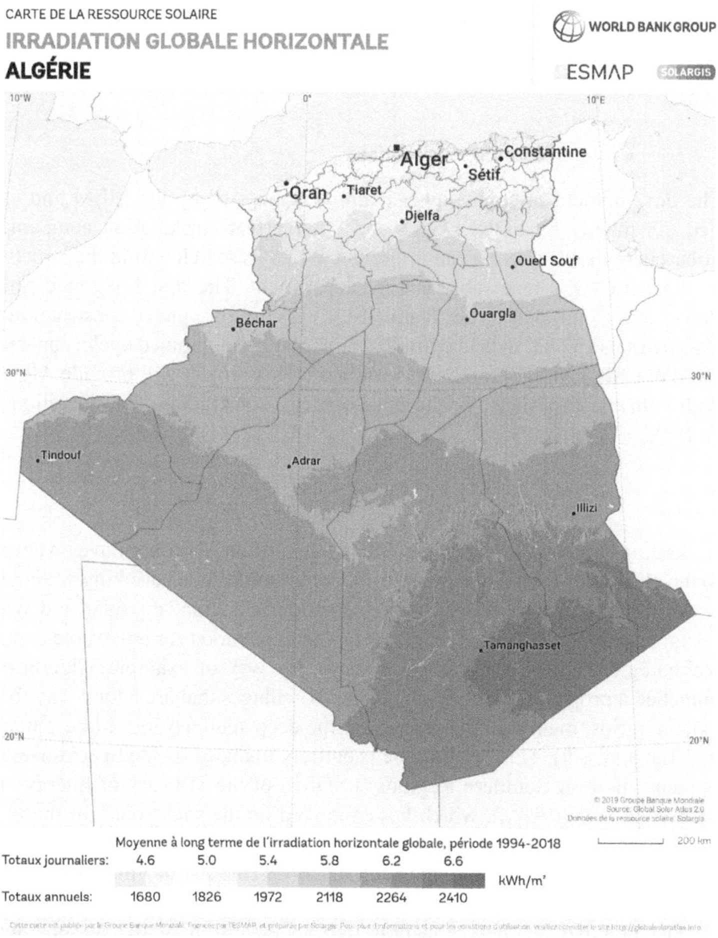

Figure 5.1 Solar potential in Algeria. Photograph by the World Bank (2021).

Algeria receives some of the highest levels of solar energy in the world every year. It amounts to around 5.2 million billion K/W/h/year.

Solar energy has the greatest potential for renewable energy in Algeria. It represents 169.44 TWh/year, or 5,000 times Algeria's electricity consumption. With more than 2,000 hours of sunshine a year, and up to 3,900 hours on the high plateaux and in the Sahara, the daily solar energy received in Algeria is around 1,700 kWh/m^2/year in the north and 2,263 kWh/m^2/year in the south, giving an average of more than 2,200 kWh/m^2/year.

Algeria plans to launch a number of solar photovoltaic projects with a total capacity of 200 MWp/year, to be implemented over the period 2021–2030. The programme for the 2021–2030 phase provides for the installation of 500 MW per year until 2023, then 600 MW per year until 2030.

5.4.1.1 *Creation of solar power plants*

The development of solar power plants is supported by the MEM and carried out mainly by SONELGAZ and other private installation companies. Solar energy is regarded as an important area of research within the structure of SONELGAZ's renewable energy department. The first Integrated Solar Power and Combined Cycle Plant (ISCC) is currently under construction at HassiR'mel (152 ha, hybrid cylindro-parabolic/gas combined cycle, capacity: 25 MW CSP, 150 MW total, €315 million). This project will provide Algeria with valuable experience in the development, construction and operation of an ISCC.

5.4.1.2 *Rural electrification using photovoltaic solar energy*

According to some estimates, more than five million Algerians have no access to the electricity grid, while many rural communities need drinking water and water for livestock or irrigation. Given Algeria's abundant solar and wind resources, these rural needs represent a potential market for renewable energy technologies (Himri et al., 2009, p. 911). By way of example, Algeria has launched a project to electrify eighteen (18) villages that are a long way from existing grids, mainly in the wilayas of the deep south (Adrar, Illizi, Tindouf and Tamanrasset). This programme is entirely financed by the Special Development Fund for Southern Regions (FSDRS) of the Ministry of Energy and Mines via SONELGAZ, which has embarked on the solar route for these 18 villages as part of the rural electrification programme with the aim of boosting the use of photovoltaic renewable energies (the list of villages is shown in Table 5.4).

The photovoltaic power stations are an extension of the diesel power stations that already exist in isolated areas, and are used for electrification, pumping, telecommunications, public lighting and small refrigeration systems

Table 5.4 Installated capacity[a] and daily domestic consumption.

Wilayas	*Village*	*Installed power (kW)*	*Consumption (kWh/day/household)*
Tamanrasset	**Moulaylahcen**	9	1.48
	Dansdelagh	15	0,92
	Tahifet	61,5	1h30
	Arak	61,5	1
	Amguid	51	1,60
	Tahernenet	30	1.13
	Étaintarabin	34,5	1.44
	Dansblel	15	1.38
Tindouf	**Garadjebilet**	33	1,47
	Jouraelkhadra	24	1,55
	Hassimounir	21	1,68
Adrar	**Hamoumoussa**	6	1,53
	Tala	16.5	1.61
Illizi	**Imehrou**	16.5	0,63
	Ifni	7.5	0,60
	Ouedpareil	15	0,68
	Tihahiout	12	0,57
	Tamadjart	24	0,80

Source: A table by The Algerian Ministry of Energy and Mines.

[a] Photovoltaic installations.

(Table 5.5). The 18 villages that benefited from these schemes were selected according to their geographical location. Located in the south, these villages have a very low population density, are isolated and far from all communication networks. As a result, their energy supply by conventional means (diesel, transport network) has shown its limitations (fuel trucking costs, catenary construction and maintenance costs, etc.). As a result, the use of decentralised photovoltaic installations enables these isolated villages to be supplied while significantly reducing the cost of transporting energy.

SONELGAZ's efforts to encourage the spread of renewable energies to sites where the production of new energy is profitable compared with conventional energy sources are aimed at making the use of renewable energies more widespread through mass production, improving the living conditions

Table 5.5 List of new concentrated solar power (CSP) Projects.

Location	*Capacity (M.W)*	*Cost (10^6 US Dollars $)*
Megahir	80	322
Naama	70	285
Hassi R'mel (II)	70	285

Source: Table by Ministry of Energy and Mines.

of isolated populations, reducing the use of hydrocarbons and gathering information on the behaviour of equipment in the Saharan environment.

NEAL is also involved in the project for rural electrification using photovoltaic solar energy. Its role is to provide financial engineering services. Private companies are also involved in rural electrification using photovoltaic solar energy. Under Law 20–02, the government is encouraging local entrepreneurs to set up businesses near villages in the south, so that they can take part in the process of producing renewable electricity (Stambouli, 2011).

Algeria has benefited from international expertise in the exploitation of photovoltaic solar energy. In this context, the Sahara region has benefited from the Sahara Solar Breeder (SSB) project (Balaska et al., 2016). A weather station has been set up in the town of Saida, at the gateway to the great Algerian Sahara Desert, to provide meteorological data for designers of new energy projects.

The performance of the various photovoltaic technologies used in Algeria has had a positive impact on energy use. For example, thanks to the use of these new photovoltaic technologies, the efficiency of solar modules has been improved, now reaching more than 40% (Green et al., 2012; cited by Balaska et al., 2016, p. 2). The use of new technologies in solar installations increases energy production in different climatic conditions and geographical locations. The choice of appropriate technology for photovoltaic installations is of paramount importance, especially for a country like Algeria, which has great potential for solar energy (Figure 5.2).

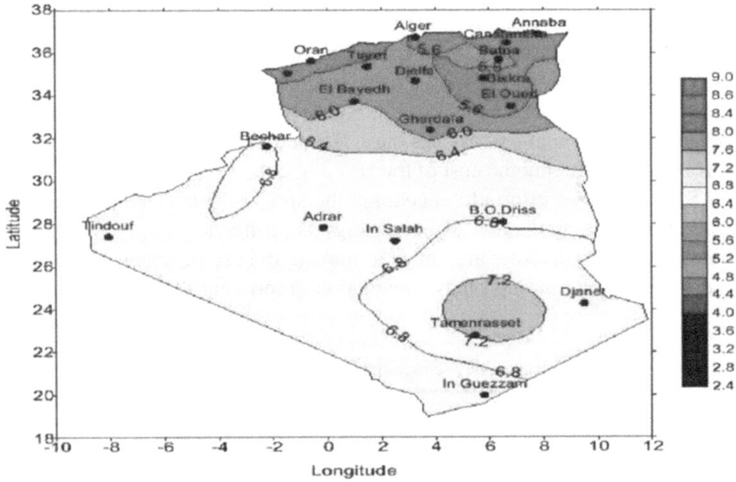

Figure 5.2 Solar electricity supply sites in North Africa*. Overall daily exposure (in kWh/m/day)². Photograph by World Bank (2021).

5.4.1.3 Concentrated Solar Power (CSP) in Algeria: The DESERTEC project

Many regions of the world are physically suited to the development of CSP, including the entire MENA region. Among these areas, the Algerian Sahara is particularly attractive for market development, given the availability of land and proximity to large, highly remunerative markets. The potential for electricity generation is enormous in relation to regional and global energy demands—around 2% of the Sahara Desert could meet global demand and 0.4% could meet European (EU) demand (DLR, 2005; Gelil, 2007; Estela, 2009; cited in Stambouli, 2011, p. 1173).

The long-term target of 20% renewable energy by 2030 is to be achieved mainly from CSP (70% CSP, 20% wind and 10% PV), which would make it one of the most ambitious CSP programmes in the world. In order to meet these ambitious targets, NEAL is implementing solar projects such as the first 25 MW solar power project in Hassi R'mel (150 MW total, CSP/natural gas), which is currently being implemented and three new projects at different stages of review.

Looking to the future, a proposal called DESERTEC has been put forward by the Trans-Mediterranean Renewable Energy Cooperation (TREC). The solar plan envisages a network linking North Africa and Europe that will harness North Africa's vast solar and wind resources to bring clean energy to Africa and Europe. Based on the DESERTEC concept, a consortium of 12 leading energy, technology and finance companies (including Munich Re, Siemens, Cevital, Deutsche Bank, RWE, EON, Schott Solar) formed a DESERTEC Industrial Initiative (DII) in October 2009, which will conduct feasibility studies and develop project plans to realise a large-scale export of solar electricity from the MENA region to Europe. At its first meeting in Munich in July 2009, the consortium outlined its intention to invest 400 billion dinars over the next 40 years to supply 15% of the European electricity market with imported solar electricity produced in CSP plants in North Africa. In the first phase, DESERTEC Industrial Initiative (DII) will focus on advocating for the opening of the EU market to MENA CSP exports. In the medium term, the programme will provide the necessary industry and government experience and market development to enable the large-scale private sector investments envisaged by DESERTEC Industrial Initiative (DII) members.

5.4.2 Wind energy

Wind power can be harnessed wherever average wind speeds exceed 5–6 m/s. Algeria has a vast wind energy development project. Studies of wind energy resources in Algeria carried out by the CDER over the last few years show that climatic conditions in Algeria are favourable to the use of wind energy.

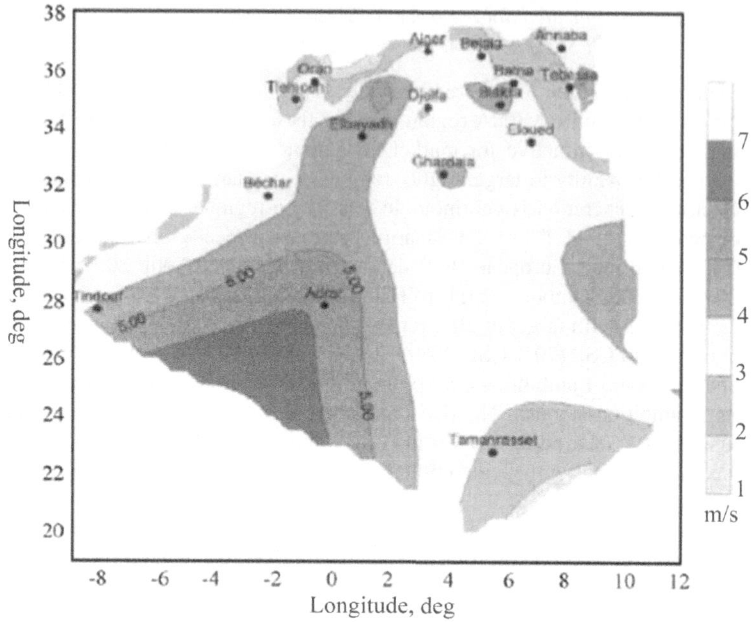

Figure 5.3 Wind map of Algeria. Photograph by the World Bank (2021).

Algeria's wind map in Figure 5.3 shows that 50% of the country's surface has a considerable average wind speed. The best wind energy potential is found in southern Algeria, particularly in the south-western region, where wind speeds exceed 6 m/s, as shown in Table 5.6, which presents the average annual wind speeds and power at three sites in the south-western region of Algeria (Adrar, Timimoun and Tindouf) (Himri et al., 2009). This energy potential is ideal for pumping water, especially in the high plains.

The wind resource has been the subject of an evaluation study by the public company Sonelgaz. There are currently six pilot electrification and telecommunications projects identified and quantified in the wilayas of Adrar,

Table 5.6 Average annual wind speed at six locations in southern Algeria.

Sites	*Adrar*	*Tindouf*	*Bordj Badji Mokhtar*	*Béchar*	*Tamanrasset*	*Djanet*
Average annual speed	6.3	5.1	4.6	4.4	3.7	3.3

Source: Table by Ministry of Energy and Mines.

Tindouf, Bordj Badji Mokhtar, Béchar, Tamanrassat and Djanet. However, the Adrar region receives the greatest quantities of wind compared with the other regions of the country. Sonelgaz's study, estimating the power that can be recovered at heights of between 10 and 50 metres, identifies this region as the most suitable site for a wind farm. Other sites in the North and the High Plateaux also offer significant energy potential. The topography and roughness of the terrain at these wind farm sites are also measured and quantified to better simulate and understand wind flow (MEM, 2005; quoted in Stambouli, 2011, p. 1174; Himri et al., 2009, p. 913).

Algeria has a moderate wind regime (2 to 6 m/s). In the north, average wind speeds are generally low. However, there are microclimates on the coastal sites of Oran, Bejaïa and Annaba, on the high plateaux of Tiaret and Kheiter and in the region bounded by Bejaïa in the north and Biskra in the south. Unlike the north, the south is characterised by higher speeds, particularly in the south-west, with speeds in excess of 4 m/s, and exceeding 6 m/s in the Adrar region (Boubou-Bouziani, 2017, p. 127).

Algeria is encouraging the use of wind energy through a series of laws and official programmes. NEAL has applied to several sources for funding and support for its projects. On the one hand, the projected objectives are part of the actions requested, supported and financed by the World Bank, the International Energy Agency (IEA) and the European Investment Bank. On the other hand, it also receives funding from the Algerian government (Himri et al., 2009, p. 915).

However, practical applications of wind energy are still limited due to high costs and the need for technological progress (Himri et al., 2009). By 2030, Algeria plans to generate almost 40% of its electricity from renewable sources. Although solar energy is the predominant choice, wind energy represents the second production axis of this programme. Energy access is widely considered to be the missing link in the Millennium Development Goals. Yet it is energy access that will enable people around the world, and especially in Algeria, to escape the poverty trap. The time has therefore come to make access to "renewable" energy a priority to promote the development of the country's economic sector (Boubou-Bouziani, 2017).

5.4.3 Algeria's hydroelectric potential

The overall flows falling on Algerian territory are significant, estimated at 65 billion cubic metres, but are of little benefit to the country: limited rainy days, concentration in limited areas, high evaporation and rapid evacuation towards the sea. Schematically, surface resources decrease from north to south. Currently, the balance of useful and renewable energy is around 25 billion cubic metres, of which around 2/3 is surface resources (Boubou-Bouziani, 2017).

In Algeria, 103 dam sites have been identified. More than 50 dams are currently operational. The share of these small-scale generating facilities is around

Table 5.7 Hydroelectric generating capacity in Algeria.

Central	*Installed capacity (MW)*
Draguina	71,5
Ighilemda	24–4
Mansoria	100
Erraguene	16
Souk El Djemaa	8,085
Tizi Meden	4,458
Ighzenchebel	2,712
Ghrib	7,000
Gouriet	6,425
Bouhanifia	5,700
Oued Fodda	15,600
Beni Behdel	3,500
Tessala	4,228
Total	286

Source: Table by Algerian Ministry of Energy and Mines (2016).

5%, complementing natural gas-fired electricity generation (Ministry of Hydrocarbons and Mines, 2005). The total capacity of 13 of these is 269.208 MW, as shown in the Table 5.7 below. At 265 GWh in 2003, hydroelectricity accounted for barely 1% of total electricity production (Stambouli, 2011).

As far as small-scale hydroelectricity is concerned, it is only possible to increase production slightly (Himri et al., 2009). Hydroelectric capacity accounts for around 4% of total electricity production, or 230 MW.[8] This low capacity is due to the insufficient number of exploitable hydraulic sites (Boubou-Bouziani, 2017).

5.4.4 *Geothermal energy*

As far as geothermal energy is concerned, there are many hot springs, but they are not exploited for industrial purposes. More than 200 geothermal springs have been counted by the Centre for the Development of Renewable Energies (CDER), and one third of them have temperatures above 45°C. The highest temperatures recorded are 98°C and 118°C in Hamam El Maskhoutin and Biskra, respectively, located in the western part of the country. Geothermal energy cannot be excluded from the electricity option of the renewable energy network. Some of these sources can be exploited to produce renewable electricity.

5.4.5 *Biomass*

The various renewable energy sources used include biomass. Biomass is a constantly growing source in Algeria, with a wide variety of compositions. Untreated waste is a significant source of pollution, particularly landfill sites, technical landfill sites, industrial waste, etc. To this end, the recovery of greenhouse gases emitted by this waste for energy purposes (in the form of biogas) should be considered (Boubou-Bouziani, 2017).

Northern Algeria accounts for 10% of the country's surface area, or 2,500,000 hectares. Forest covers 1,800,000 hectares and degraded scrubland 1,900,000 hectares. Maritime pine and eucalyptus are particularly interesting plants for energy use, although they currently occupy only 5% of Algeria's forest. Algeria's biomass potential is made up of biomass from forests (around 37 Mtoe, with a potential recovery rate of around 10%), urban and agricultural waste (estimated at 1.33 Mtoe/year, i.e., 5 million tonnes not recycled.[9] As part of any plan to develop waste treatment and energy recovery for biofuel production in Algeria, an inventory of waste and biomass needs to be drawn up (Boubou-Bouziani, 2017).

5.4.6 Biogas

Biogas is produced by the anaerobic fermentation of organic animal or plant matter. It occurs spontaneously in landfill sites for municipal waste, but it can also be produced artificially in enclosures called "digesters" in which solid or liquid organic waste and the bacterial cultures needed for this transformation are introduced (Boubou-Bouziani, 2017). It represents an energy potential that is still very poorly exploited in Algeria. By way of example, biogas from the El Karma wastewater treatment plant (wilaya of Oran) is recovered from an anaerobic digestion process, at a rate of $150m^3/H$. This is currently used to heat the digesters, using special boilers, while the surplus is flared to avoid atmospheric pollution with methane gas, which makes up 70% of biogas compared with other gases. A biogas cogeneration study is being carried out by the Ministry for electrical recovery (Boubou-Bouziani, 2017).

5.4.7 The national programme for the development of renewable energy and energy efficiency

Implementing this ambitious programme will require colossal investments estimated at 120 billion dollars, given its objective of achieving an estimated 40% share of renewable energies in the energy mix by 2030. The RE programme (2011–2030) is defined in four phases:

- 2011–2013: Facility with a total capacity of 110 MW
- 2014–2015: Installed capacity of 650 MW
- 2016–2020: Installed capacity is expected to reach around 2,600 MW, with an export potential of 2,000 MW
- Additional capacity of around 12,000 MW should be installed by 2030, with the possibility of exporting up to 10,000 MW.

Table 5.8 Breakdown by sector of the national renewable energy programme (2015–2030).

Unit: MW	*2015–2020*	*2021–2030*	*Total*
Photovoltaic	3000	10575	13575
Wind	1010	4000	5010
CSP	–	2000	2000
Cogeneration	150	250	400
Biomass	360	640	1000
Geothermal	5	10	15
Total	4525	17475	22000

Source: Table by the Algerian Ministry of Energy.

Renewable energy capacity will be installed according to the specific features and characteristics of each region (Atmania & Salem, 2019):

- Southern region: for the hybridisation of existing power stations and the supply of power to scattered sites, given the importance of solar and wind potential and the availability of space, which favours this region;
- The high plateaux region: for its sun and wind potential, with the possibility of acquiring land;
- Coastal region: depending on the availability of land, with all areas such as roofs and terraces of buildings and other unused areas being exploited. Additional requirements for other areas of application are included in the total photovoltaic capacity, such as residential, agriculture, pumping, water resources, industry, public lighting and services.

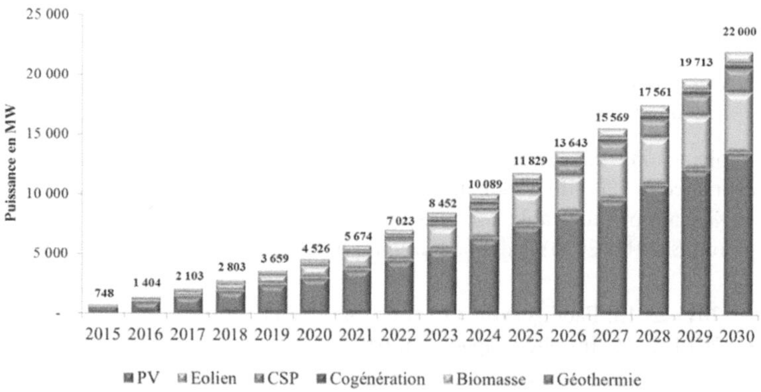

Figure 5.4 Breakdown by sector of the national renewable energy programme (2015–2030). Diagram by the Algerian Ministry of Energy.

Renewable energy projects to produce electricity for the national market will be carried out in two stages: the first stage, from 2015 to 2020, envisages the construction of 4010 MW of photovoltaic and wind power, and 515 MW of biomass, cogeneration and geothermal power. The second stage runs from 2021 to 2030. The development of the interconnection between the North and the Sahara (Adrar) will enable the installation of large-scale renewable energy plants in the regions of Ain Salah, Adrar, Timimoune and Bechar, and their integration into the national energy system.

The renewable energy programme to be implemented for the national market over the period 2015–2030 is 22,000 MW, broken down by sector as follows in the Table 5.8 and Figure 5.4.

5.5 Difficulties and obstacles in implementing the national renewable energy and energy efficiency programme

A few years after launching the programme, the results are proving to be very modest and insufficient (production of 400 MW from RE instead of the 650 MW planned in the programme for 2015). In 2015, 14 photovoltaic power plants with an installed capacity of 268 MW were commissioned in the High Plateaux and southern Algeria. These achievements are still very low, given Algeria's huge solar potential (it has one of the largest solar deposits in the world, with over 3,500 hours of sunshine a year), which is unfortunately not being properly exploited. The efforts made are proving insufficient to exploit the full potential available in Algeria. The 2000–2020 balance sheet remains very modest and reflects the shortcomings of an approach whose consequences we are now suffering.

5.5.1 Barriers and constraints of the approach

We must not overlook the fact that, as in many other countries, the deployment of renewable energies in Algeria comes up against multiple constraints and barriers, namely economic, technical, institutional and socio-cultural barriers (Benaouag & Rahmani, 2019).

5.5.1.1 Economic barriers

Economic barriers represent real obstacles to the promotion of RE in Algeria (Benaouag & Rahmani, 2019):

- The structure of the electricity market is characterised by the state monopoly on production and distribution, in addition to the low price of electricity, which is subsidised in Algeria.

- The high cost of RE technologies means that the price of the energy they produce is very high, which constitutes a barrier to entry into the electricity market.
- The lack of public or private sector funding for investment in RE. Indeed, despite the efforts made in Algeria in terms of RE funding, the amounts allocated remain insufficient compared with other countries such as India and Morocco.
- The failure of the market to internalise the cost of negative externalities in the price of electricity (resulting from the use of conventional methods of electricity production, such as pollution, greenhouse gases, etc.).

5.5.1.2 Technical (technological) barriers

These barriers are linked to research and development activities in the RE. In the case of Algeria, they mainly concern:

- Lack of funding for research institutes to develop RE technologies;
- The risks and uncertainty surrounding the design, installation and performance of certain technologies;
- The very high cost of producing new technologies, which limits their use and spread.
- The lack of skills needed to develop, manufacture and maintain technologies;
- In Algeria, unlike solar energy, wind power cannot be developed on a large scale because most regions are not very exposed to the wind.

5.5.1.3 Institutional barriers

These barriers are of a strategic, regulatory or political nature for the development and promotion of RE (Margolis & Zuboy, 2006). Algerian public authorities have had to review RE policy for the following reasons:

- Ambiguity of strategies and public policies;
- Lack or absence of regulations for the management of the RE sector;
- The bureaucracy of the administrations in charge of these issues;
- Inadequate administrative procedures;
- Stakeholders not involved in promoting RE.

5.5.1.4 Socio-cultural barriers

These barriers also constitute real constraints to the dissemination of RE and concern in particular:

- Households are not sufficiently informed about the negative environmental impacts and costs/benefits of using each type of technology.

- Lack of incentives for consumers to use RE.
- A lack of concern for pollution and environmental issues due to society's lack of awareness of these issues.
- The low level of household power affects the choice of spending priorities.

5.5.2 The lack of ambition in Algeria's energy conservation and efficiency policy

Furthermore, the difficulties and obstacles encountered in implementing the national renewable energy and energy efficiency programme lie in the lack of coordination between the various sectors, the shortage of local technical skills and the non-compliance of current financing methods.

In other words, the limits of the current approach to the development of renewable energies relate to the problem of compartmentalisation and cross-sector coordination, which is sometimes non-existent. In this case, it is vital to strengthen cross-sector synergies to achieve greater convergence in the energy transition and the development of renewable energies.

Another factor to be taken into account when developing renewable energies will be the synergy of skills. It is important to break down the barriers between different sectors (energy, energy transition, industry, environment, etc.). The solar photovoltaic industry is lagging far behind in Algeria.

Most industrial projects in the field of renewable energies are experiencing delays in their implementation. The prospects for the local solar photovoltaic kit production industry require international technological know-how and production resources across the value chain in solar photovoltaic devices (solar photovoltaic panels, batteries and inverters).

To ensure that this renewable energy industry gets off to a good start in Algeria, it makes sense to move towards a national and international public-private partnership.

Furthermore, the biggest challenge to the proper development of the renewable energy (RE) sector in Algeria will be to put in place a genuine training and maintenance policy in the field of renewable energy.

In the 1980s, the Ministry of Energy drew up an energy model, the main aim of which was to rationalise energy consumption and develop alternative energies, in this case LPG and renewable energies. In 1980, electricity production was 1,800 MW, rising to more than 22,000 MW in 2020 and expected to reach 30,000 MW by 2030 (Ministry of Energy). At the end of December 2021, installed renewable energy capacity stood at 567.1 MW, 438.2 MW of which was non-hydro. The year 1999 also saw the drafting of the law on energy management, followed by the law on thermal insulation of buildings in 2000. Very little has been achieved between 2000 and 2020 in terms of developing renewable energies, energy saving and energy efficiency.

The legislative and regulatory texts enacted to promote energy policy do not provide sufficient detail on the support methods and incentives to be granted to investors and industrial companies wishing to become involved in the various renewable energy sectors. Moreover, in the world ranking of countries according to the WEF "Renewable Energy Regulation Index" (2019), Algeria compares unfavourably with the Maghreb countries. Algeria is in 77th place behind Tunisia (21st) and Morocco (36th), but also in relation to countries such as Egypt (40th) and Jordan (41st).

The widespread use of new energies by households, businesses and public administrations bears witness to this lack of policy ambition in Algeria. The challenge for the public authorities is to fill these gaps by increasing investment linked directly and indirectly to renewable energies.

5.6 Conclusion

At the end of the day, Algeria's renewable energy potential is dominated by solar energy, compared with wind, biomass, geothermal and hydroelectric power. To make the most of this scarce resource, the government has made the development of renewable energies a central objective of its energy policy.

As part of its energy "strategies," Algeria has mobilised a number of instruments as part of its policy to develop renewable energies, which provide a framework for investment in the energy sector and contribute directly or indirectly to its development and growth.

However, the level of Algeria's commitment to harnessing new energies remains below the country's potential, as demonstrated by the level of production and consumption of this energy and the state of the energy industry, which is still at the start-up stage.

Catching up with Algeria's lag in renewable energy investment requires progress on several fronts. On the supply side, the public authorities need to promote the widespread use of new energies by households, businesses and public institutions (local authorities, administration, etc.). On the demand side, the mobilisation of new energy technologies can have a positive impact on the process of energy use.

However, it should be stressed that in view of the overall context in which the national economy is evolving, several aspects of which have been highlighted in the previous chapters and in this one, the obstacles to the development of renewable energies in Algeria are so powerful that it is difficult to envisage a successful energy transition in Algeria. In conclusion, the discourse and actions undertaken by the State on the question of renewable energies are, at best, a communication operation for international opinion, at worst, a new channel for distributing income through projects with no future. In other words, there is every indication that the public authorities want to turn the rhetoric on the need to move beyond rents into rents.

Notes

1 For more information on this institution, visit the website of the Algerian National Agency for the Promotion and Rationalisation of Energy Use (APRUE). https://www.aprue.org.dz/index.php/fr/presentation/creation
2 For more details, see: World Bank (2009). Energy in the Middle East and North Africa. Report No. 48329-MNA. Washington, DC: World Bank Group, 2009.
3 Minor changes affecting the operation and organisation of the Renewable Energy and Energy Efficiency Commission (CEREFE) were made in Executive Decree no. 21–95 of 10 March 2021 amending and supplementing Executive Decree no. 19–280 of 20 October 2019 on the creation, organisation and operation of the Renewable Energy and Energy Efficiency Commission (this text of the law can be accessed on the website: https://faolex.fao.org/docs/pdf/alg210046.pdf).
4 United Nations Commission on Sustainable Development (2011). Algeria National Report, 19ème session of the United Nations Commission on Sustainable Development (CSD-19), May 2011, 42 pages.
5 According to the Algerian Ministry of Energy and Mines, SONATRACH (an acronym for "Société nationale pour la recherche, la production, le transport, la transformation, et la commercialisation des hydrocarbures") is an Algerian oil and gas company. It was founded on 31 December 1963. It is a major player in the oil industry, nicknamed the "African Major." Sonatrach is ranked as the leading company in Africa (for more information, visit the website of the Algerian Ministry of Energy and Mines https://www.energy.gov.dz/ or the website of the state-owned company Sonatrach https://sonatrach.com/).
6 According to the Algerian Ministry of Energy and Mines, SONELGAZ (an acronym for Société nationale de l'électricité et du gaz) is an Algerian industrial energy group specialising in the production, distribution and marketing of electricity and the purchase, transport, distribution and marketing of natural gas. Its head office is in Algiers. SONELGAZ is the leading electricity producer and supplier and the leading gas distributor in Algeria. It supplies electricity to 10 million customers and gas to 6 million (Ministry of Energy and Mines-Algeria). For more information, please visit the website of the Ministry of Energy and Mines (Algeria): https://www.energy.gov.dz/ or that of the public company SONELGAZ: https://www.sonelgaz.dz/fr).
7 Sunshine, also known as **insolation**, is the measure of solar radiation received by a surface over a given period, expressed in megajoules per square metre, MJ/m^2 (as recommended by the World Meteorological Organisation) or in watt-hours per square metre, Wh/m^2 (mainly used by the solar industry). This measurement divided by the recording time provides a measure of power density, known as irradiance, expressed in watts per square metre (W/m).[2]
8 "Produire plus propre", Centre National des Technologies de Production plus Propre, Ministère de l'aménagement du territoire et de l'environnement, No. 08, May-June 2011.
9 "Produire plus propre", Centre National des Technologies de Production plus Propre, Ministère de l'aménagement du territoire et de l'environnement, No. 08, May-June 2011.

References

African Energy Commission (AFREC). (2023). *Africa energy balances: French edition.* African Energy Commission. https://au-afrec.org/sites/default/files/2023-09/Africa%20Energy%20Balances%20French%20edition%20RGB%20%281%29.pdf

Atmania, H., & Salem, A. (2019). L'investissement dans les énergies renouvelables en Algérie, un pas vers la transition énergétique (cas de l'énergie solaire). Revue algérienne d'économie et gestion, 12(1), 151–167. https://asjp.cerist.dz/en/article/82240

Balaska, A., Tahri, A., Stambouli, A. B., Tahri, F., & Oozeki, T. (2016, March). Comparative performance evaluation of different technologies of photovoltaic modules in Algeria. In: 2016 7th International Renewable Energy Congress (IREC). IEEE, 2016. pp. 1–5.

Benaouag, C., & Rahmani, M. (2019). Les barrières au développement des énergies renouvelables en Algérie. Stratégie et développement, 9(3), 261–273.

Boubou-Bouziani, N. (2017). Potentiel et développement des énergies renouvelables en Algérie. Communication Science & Technology, 19, 120–132.

Gelil, A. I. (2007). Framework Conditions for Solar Thermal Energy Use in the Southern Mediterranean Countries SOLATERM Project Report.

Himri, Y., Stambouli, A. B., Draoui, B., & Himri, S. (2009). Review of wind energy use in Algeria. Renewable and Sustainable Energy Reviews, 13(4), 910–914.

Margolis, R., & Zuboy, J. (2006). Nontechnical barriers to solar energy use: Review of recent literature. Office of Scientific and Technical Information (OSTI). https://doi.org/10.2172/893639

Ministry of Hydrocarbons and Mines. (2005). *Bilan énergétique national: Année 2005.* Ministry of Hydrocarbons and Mines. https://www.energy.gov.dz/?article=bilan-energetique-national-du-secteur

Ministry of Hydrocarbons and Mines. (2016). *Bilan énergétique national: Année 2016.* Ministry of Hydrocarbons and Mines. https://www.energy.gov.dz/?article=bilan-energetique-national-du-secteur

Stambouli, A. B. (2011). Promotion of renewable energies in Algeria: Strategies and perspectives. Renewable and sustainable energy reviews, 2011, vol. 15, no 2, p. 1169–1181.

General conclusion

In the introduction, we highlighted the methodological difficulties that economists in particular encounter when analysing the field of market activities in Algeria. These difficulties stem from the nature of the regulatory rationality that governs the allocation of wealth flows in this country. In an area where the economy has yet to emancipate itself from politics, and where rents dominate relations between the state and society, the choice of approach to adopt becomes problematic. The example of the limits of economics and political science is instructive in this respect. We also emphasised the desirability of using the notion of extractivism to remedy this difficulty. This concept, by virtue of the breadth of its object of study, makes it possible to overcome the compartmentalisation between the various social science disciplines, and is part of a multidisciplinary approach likely to cover several aspects, hitherto neglected, of the "phenomenon" of rents.

The analysis of Algerian economic history, inspired by the eclectic approach of "extractivism," has enabled us to better identify the reasons for the persistence of the rentier and extractivist character in Algeria. This fact is fundamentally political, given the characteristics of the Algerian politico-economic system discussed throughout this study.

This system obeys an overall logic whose continuity has not been called into question by the many changes at the head of state, nor by the various economic reform movements undertaken since the early 1980s. Beyond the spectacular reversals that have been observed from time to time, the system remains fundamentally unchanged: the embedding of the economic sphere in the political sphere, and the use of economic resources to maintain power, are among the constants that symbolise the continuity of the system despite the many changes it has undergone, particularly over the last four decades. This state of affairs sums up the ambiguity of the Algerian political system, which, on the one hand, seeks to wipe out the many deficits that sterilise oil revenues and, on the other, does not want to give up using the economy to dominate society.

As a result, the question of economic reform in Algeria oscillates, depending on the situation, between a political discourse advocating reform and

DOI: 10.4324/9781003665571-7

economic practices that produce and accentuate deficits. In this respect, three important observations should be made:

First, the correlation between the initiation (and cessation) of reforms and the inflow of foreign currency into the state coffers has always been verified. In fact, whether at the end of the 1980s or in the mid-1990s, it was always the level of oil revenues that dictated the resumption or abandonment of economic reforms. It is easy to see that as soon as the rise in world hydrocarbon prices took hold, the Algerian government abandoned the idea of economic reform. Instead, the official discourse is one of economic recovery, as if the crisis in the Algerian economy had only been temporary.

Second, no reform experiment has been completed, including the structural adjustment programme, even though it was implemented under the supervision of the IMF and Algeria's traditional creditors (EU, USA, etc.). They were all halted halfway through without any assessment or public debate on their results. Finally, all the reform projects that have been initiated have come from the political regime, which, since the 1980s, has been the sole initiator of the reforms and the first to call them into question. Paradoxical as it may seem, the State, or the political regime that invested it, is the first and main obstacle to the successful transition of Algeria to a productive market economy.

Finally, thanks to oil revenues, the political regime became autonomous and exercised domination over civil society, preventing its formation in several ways:

By virtue of the political ideology that drives it, the Algerian government is obsessed with confiscating all the powers of society, the most important of which is economic power. Nationalisation during the period of centralised planning and state control of access to the market after the "reforms" are part of this approach. In this sense, rents enabled the regime not to depend on taxation, and therefore on a productive economy. In so doing, it prevents the emergence of productive and enterprising social strata by favouring those who reproduce by capturing the rent.

On the political front, the government is protecting itself against the emergence of competing and autonomous political forces from civil society by simply banning all political activity, corruption and violence. The proliferation of scandals, mainly in the financial sphere and in public procurement, the denial of freedom of political and trade union representation, the ban on public demonstrations and the massive violations of human rights, whether in the 1990s or during and after the "*Hirak*" of 22 February 2019, are symptomatic signs of this.

Finally, the government is promoting the cultural impoverishment of society by encouraging the spread of backward-looking ideas through schools, which some describe as a disaster area. The aim is to maintain a community spirit in which the individual has no place.

These practices have led to an intense and perverse relationship between the formal sphere and the informal one, with the latter benefiting politically and/or economically.

In political terms, the system's framework is made up of two power structures: on the one hand, there are informal institutions with real power and formal institutions with no effective authority. In this case, the formal institutions are reduced to sounding boards for the strategies of the actors operating in the informal sector.

On the economic front, the structuring of the national market on the basis of scarcity and rent, encouraged by the neo-patrimonial nature of the political system, gave rise to predation, corruption and the development of the so-called informal or parallel economy. It was far from being a marginal phenomenon, since it covered all sectors of activity and, in just a few decades, became the real channel for capturing the income that the State distributed to buy the social peace on which the survival of the political regime depended. In this sense, the informal sector is really questioning the "*nature of the State*."

The junction between these two spheres has led to the total paralysis of the formal institutions of the State, producing a climate of complacency, of rentier behaviour, of a reversal of the scale of values to the detriment of the notion of work, of non-citizenship, of the proliferation of political delinquency and of social violence? In a word, the total decay of state institutions. In this climate, the idea of abandoning the rentier and extractivist nature of the economy for the sake of a productive market economy in Algeria meets with extreme resistance. These forces are not opposed to the reforms that the State would have liked to initiate; they are the ones nestling in the institutions of the State and dictating the conduct of the country's economic policies.

Index